debt

Life after debt

WOMEN'S SURVIVAL STORIES

Sue Wells

Scarlet Press

For my daughters Catherine, Anna and Sophie.
May they always live in abundance.

Published by Scarlet Press
5 Montague Road, London E8 2HN

Copyright © Sue Wells 1997

The author assert her moral right to be identified as the author of this work in accordance with the Copyright, Design and Patents Act 1988

British Library Cataloguing-in-Publication Data
A catalogue record for this book is available from the British Library
ISBN 1 85727 043 6 pb

All rights reserved. No part of this publication may be reproduced or transmitted in any form or by any means, electronic or mechanical, including photocopying, recording, or any information storage and retrieval system, without permission in writing from the publisher.

Designed and produced for Scarlet Press by
Chase Production Services, Chadlington, OX7 3LN
Typeset from the author's disk by
Stanford Desktop Publishing Services, Northampton
Printed in the EC by J.W. Arrowsmith Ltd, Bristol

Contents

Acknowledgements   vii

Introduction   viii

Part One: Women's Survival Stories   1

1: Perspectives on the lives of women in debt   3

2: Separation or divorce   21
   Jennifer: house repossession   21
   Laura: divorce and failure to secure child
     maintenance payments   33
   Emily: a 'battered' wife becomes independent   43
   Alice: pension rights in divorce settlements   50

3: Loans and grants   59
   Isobel: single-parent student who survived   59
   Lisa: single-parent student who did not survive   67

4: Business failure   77
   Rebecca: bankruptcy, repossession and
     more debts   77
   Josephine: bankruptcy, repossession and
     survival   89

5: Personal addictions   99
   Margaret: heroin, motherhood and abstinence   99
   Mary: shopping, shopping and bankruptcy   112

Part Two: Managing Debt Positively   125

6: Women and debt   127

7:	How to get the most out of your income	134
8:	Losing your job	137
9:	Mortgage repayments and house repossession	139
10:	Loans and grants	146
11:	Having a baby	149
12:	Separation and divorce	155
13:	Single parents: maximising income	170
14:	Benefits for parents on low pay	174
15:	Business debts	177
16:	Credit cards and credit agreements	182
17:	Bankruptcy: three women's experiences	186
18:	Being a student	189

Resources 194
Useful organisations 200
Useful publications 205

Acknowledgements

I want to thank all the women who contributed their experiences to this book with honesty, openness and trust. This includes those whose stories do not appear for various reasons but whose contributions towards a better understanding of what it is like for women to be in debt are none the less valuable.

I also thank all the agencies and organisations who have responded so readily with helpful information and in particular Alicia Webster at the Bristol Citizen's Advice Bureau and the Child Poverty Action Group who kindly forwarded me some invaluable publications free of charge. I shall now donate these to Bristol CAB.

I also want to thank my husband Martin for his support, encouragement and unfailing willingness to help me when it was needed. My daughters too have been a source of encouragement, even when they wanted to use the computer themselves. I also want to thank my friends, especially Ken and Elizabeth Mellor, for their inspiration and Angie Sage, who has followed the book's progress with interest and enthusiasm.

Introduction

Money, like sex, is a private matter. But while people's sexual problems seem to be aired all over the place, their money problems are not. Debt often remains a secret, even between couples and friends, or within families. It is often associated with shame, blame, failure and guilt. We sometimes read about men in serious debt committing suicide. These men are often from middle- or upper-class backgrounds or have a notoriously stressful occupation. But what about women in debt? How do they cope with similar pressures? Do their particular backgrounds or occupations influence how they respond to being in debt?

The idea of debt – or being in debt – has always been rather chilling. So many of us live – or have lived – on the breadline, lurching from one pay packet to the next, scratching around for bargains in the supermarket or making a special trip to get something cheaper elsewhere. After all, we are usually in charge of the family purse when it comes to buying household stuff. But what happens when we begin to overspend? When does it become a problem – and when is it recognised as such? Should it become serious, does it then become a personality problem or an illness?

I know someone who has been seriously in debt for years. I got used to hearing that her telephone or electricity supply had been cut off, that she had no money for food, but knew that she was, at the same time, surrounded by beautiful and expensive things. I didn't take much notice until she had a child. It was then that moral indignation crept in. How could she allow this or that to happen, now that she was a mother? Surely she wanted to do things differently now? Her debts grew and grew until eventually she lost her house. Her anxiety was profound. It kept her awake at nights. It took over her whole life. The prospect of being rehoused by the council was grim and decidedly unattractive. The few thousand pounds she was eventually left with after a

Introduction

miraculous, last-minute sale in an effort to beat off the bailiffs, ran like sand through her fingers in a very short time. She has never sought help, apart from legal assistance. I don't think she sees debt as a problem, because she has never really faced it. This seems to be a turning point for the women in debt to whom I spoke: getting help.

What is it like being a woman in debt? How does it affect women, their families and friends, and the communities in which they live? What does debt do to a woman? I decided to talk to some women in debt – women from different backgrounds whose experiences of debt differed widely. I wanted to find out what debt meant to them, how they managed it and whether or not there were similarities in the ways in which they coped. What, if anything, about women makes their situation different from that of men? Are their debts attributable to any experiences held in common, specific to women?

The book is written primarily for women facing debt – either those trying to help themselves or those getting help through an agency. Part One, 'Women's Survival Stories', is a selection of case histories, and Part Two, 'Managing Debt Positively', gives practical advice and information on the benefits to which they – and women in similar positions – might be entitled. Almost all the women to whom I spoke about being in debt said that they wished they had known of somewhere to go for help when they needed it. A number also said that the professional advice they got was not always sound. This book is therefore also aimed at those professionally involved in helping women in financial crises better to understand the particular issues that women face and the needs that arise out of them.

The women whose stories appear in the book differ in terms of age, educational background, class and location. They are mostly white and British. I got to know them through various organisations and institutions as well as through personal contacts. They are at different stages in terms of resolving their debt problems. Some have not yet done so, most have. Perhaps the major difficulty for many women in debt is the essential initial phase: recognising that they need help and that their experience is not unique. I hope this book will enable them to acknowledge this, and to realise that we all benefit from shared experience.

Another reason for writing this book is to promote more openness in talking about financial difficulties so that, as with sexual problems, people can feel OK about asking for help.

Debt is a problem that is escalating. On the one hand women are encouraged to spend, take out loans, consume. Yet we are not often taught how to budget, economise, plan our finances. Nevertheless we are expected, at the very least, to manage household budgets and not plunge the family into debt – to cope financially regardless of pressures in relationships or the workplace, often with inadequate incomes. I hope this book will both demonstrate the need to understand the effect of these pressures and expectations on women – especially on women in debt – and emphasise the value of education in personal finance as part of daily living.

Part One

Women's Survival Stories

1 Perspectives on the lives of women in debt

This section of the book looks in detail at the lives of ten women in debt and the effects that this experience has had on them and their families and friends. It examines their reactions to being in debt and the ways in which they tried to cope. What did getting into debt mean to them? Did it elicit particular feelings and if so which feelings, and how did they deal with them? Did it affect their physical health or psychological well-being? Were these women able to share their problems among family and friends or get support for themselves? Did they feel that there were specific issues that affected women in debt and did they feel that their gender affected the sort of responses they got from professionals? What options did they have at the time and were they adequate? Did they seek professional help and, if so, at what stage? With hindsight would they have done things differently?

Their stories reflect many influences, including the current economic climate, which I have mentioned only briefly and in the simplest terms. Paternalistic attitudes to women and money – particularly to women in debt – are also powerful influences on how women are regarded, not only by men but also by themselves. In addition, threaded through many of their lives is the influence of the traditional role that women occupied until quite recently in relation to money.

What does it mean to be in debt?

Borrowing money is a perfectly respectable thing to do. It is endorsed by governments, enshrined in legislation and is the cornerstone of business. Many business deals and transactions depend on people borrowing money in order to buy their goods or services. Debt becomes a problem only when there is little or no prospect of it being repaid within a prescribed time limit. It then becomes a 'bad' debt.

Getting into debt usually happens because of an unexpected change of circumstances beyond the person's control: they lose their job or their partner, or interest rates rise. Debt is on the increase. More than a million people each year contact money advice organisations in the UK for help, and the number is steadily increasing. Such a vast number tends to mask the individual trauma of being in debt and the devastation that can result when people are no longer able to pay what they owe. Thousands struggle to survive without their gas and electricity, others are forced to go without a water supply; families lose their possessions to the bailiffs and, tragically, about a thousand homes a week are currently repossessed – the highest rate for two and a half years, according to recent newspaper reports. Businesses collapse, sometimes resulting in bankruptcy as well as the loss of the family home because it was put up as a guarantee against the business failing. Some people are fined or imprisoned, many of them women.

The economic background

Some blame the banks for lending too much money too easily – especially in the 1980s – others blame the economy. The consumer credit boom of the 1980s, rising interest rates and unemployment have all contributed to the increasing problem of debt. The collapse in the housing market has also affected one and a half million households, caught in the negative equity trap: the value of their property has decreased dramatically since they bought it and is currently worth considerably less than they paid for it.

Individual factors

Individual factors like redundancy, ill-health or the break-up of a relationship can also have a profound effect on people's ability to continue meeting their financial obligations. The women I interviewed for this book had all experienced a change in their personal circumstances that triggered a debt crisis: their relationships with their partners broke down, their businesses failed, they became students, they developed personal addictions. These difficulties – set against a background of government policy increasingly designed to discourage a dependency culture – have meant that financial help for many people in these circumstances has been considerably reduced, thus fuelling their debt problems. One recent example is cuts in Income Support for mortgage interest payments, providing less financial help to home owners at a time when they most need it. Reduced financial help means that these home owners are unable to prevent their arrears from escalating, which inevitably plunges them further into debt.

Women and debt

What is the impact of debt on individuals and families – and particularly on women? Why is there so little research material available? Is it the problem or the subject that is not taken seriously enough to warrant more research, or is the crucial issue how we view women and debt? Women, it seems, are often caught up in the paternalistic double standards that continue to operate in attitudes towards them: on the one hand they are expected not to know very much about dealing with money, and on the other to manage the household budget satisfactorily and not to plunge the family into debt.

A lot of pressure to spend money is exerted on women through advertising. They are exhorted to buy this or that product to improve the quality of their lives, their family's health, their sex appeal, their looks and so on. Women usually hold the purse strings when it comes to their family's needs. But what happens to those female consumers who are unable to match their spending or borrowing with their ability to repay?

Women and business

The experiences of the women in business whose stories appear in this book – and particularly those of Rebecca, whose clothing business ultimately failed – are that as women they encountered a lot of prejudice. Both Rebecca and another business woman called Josephine felt that, as women, they were not expected to understand business. Rebecca thought that this was a heavy burden to carry and that it influenced the way in which men in particular dealt with her. She also noticed that as a woman in business it was often difficult to get a point across and to keep faith with herself in a predominantly male world – 'a mere woman against this all-male might'. Although she had produced this 'being' – her clothing company – and knew exactly what she wanted for it, others, namely her predominantly male board of directors, later had the right to impose their conditions upon that 'being', which ultimately failed to survive.

Josephine's experience of prejudice was ironically a positive one and ultimately worked in her favour. She and her partner had put up their house as collateral in a joint business venture that failed. Her solicitor was able to demonstrate that the bank had not fulfilled its proper duty to Josephine in that it did not fully explain to her at the time of the 'agreement' the consequences of putting her house up as a guarantee against business failure. As a result, she was eventually able to keep her half of the house.

Finance is largely a male preserve. Women tend not to discuss money issues or their latest investments or speculate on the stock exchange. We are likely to be more easily bamboozled by jargon. We tend not to pursue financial careers, and if we do we are less likely than men to become bank managers, financial brokers or speculators. Even prostitutes – and their potentially high earnings – are usually 'managed' by males.

Women in debt

The paternalistic attitudes that exist towards women in business are at their most punitive when applied to women in debt. But while the attitude to women in business was often experienced by my interviewees as paternalistic and patronising, there was at the same time an underlying expectation that women can and should be able to cope with money – at least to some degree. The attitude to women who are in debt, however, reflects a growing climate of harshness towards them. As a result of failing to pay her fines Julie, a prostitute whom I interviewed for this book but whose story does not appear in it, was imprisoned (with her baby) for three months. Most of the female prisoners incarcerated with her had no previous convictions. They were imprisoned simply because they were unable to pay their fines, often for their television licences (in 1994 women who failed to buy a television licence constituted 77 per cent of all women fined). Each day in Britain, more than 60 people are sent to prison for failure to pay fines that are often very trivial.[1] Most are women. Non-payment of fines accounts for about one-third of women sent to prison. There are now more women in prison than ever before. Official forecasts expect the number to rise by about 10 per cent next year. The cost to the tax payer is high, but the emotional cost is much higher as many of these women are mothers and their children have to be accommodated in local authority care, often without any warning. 'Most of these women are in prison because they cannot afford to live in the normal way,' said Julie.

Poverty

Poverty is one reason people are unable 'to live in the normal way' and many live in poverty as a result of debt. It is a vicious circle: people cannot afford goods or services, and they are then fined often disproportionately large amounts, thus forcing them further into debt. If they then fail to pay their fines they go to prison – treatment that is reminiscent of Victorian times which means that those least able to pay are those most likely to be imprisoned. It seems that women are being punished more severely than men when it comes to mismanagement of money.

Expectations of women

Women are clearly expected to continue managing the household budget properly and to keep the family out of debt. This expectation does not take account of the sheer inadequacy of state benefits on which so many mothers are forced to try and survive. There is no account taken of the unexpected, like the cost of replacing a cooker, and the Social Fund which was meant for this very purpose is grossly inadequate. Welfare claimants who apply for loans to buy necessities such as beds and cookers were being turned away at a rate of about 100,000 a week in November 1994.[2] Borrowing from it is discretionary and claimants have no automatic rights, making them vulnerable to hire purchase schemes, loan sharks and so on. More than two-thirds of the Social Fund's payments are in the form of loans rather than grants. More than 200,000 grant applications were rejected outright in 1994 because they were considered to be of insufficient priority. And yet the onus on women to manage the household budget adequately is demonstrated by the fact that the number fined by magistrates has risen sharply over the last four years from 114,000 to 134,000. A third of these women were jailed because they had been unable to pay their fines for offences that would not originally have merited a prison sentence. They are mostly being fined and imprisoned because of an inadequate household budget.

Cuts in benefits to single parents

Ninety per cent of the UK's 1.6 million lone parents are women and a conservative estimate suggests that about one in six of these lives in poverty. And yet in their last budget, the same Conservative government which promoted family welfare decided to cut allowances to single parents, providing further evidence of double standards towards women and reinforcing the expectation that they will somehow cope. Those who depend on benefit and are most disadvantaged were also often held by that same Conservative government to be responsible for society's social ills. Improving living standards was not regarded by them as a way of helping the nation's poor. The immediate impact on women was impossible to assess because the Conservative government – unlike the Australian, Canadian or South African governments – refused to publish the gender impact of its economic policies. Nevertheless, it is most often women who bear the brunt of cuts in fiscal policy – particularly cuts in benefits, on which they tend to depend more substantially than do men.[3]

The newly elected Labour government's proposals to end Child Benefit for 16- to 18-year-olds risk pushing more than 500,000 families into poverty. Recent research by the Child Poverty Action Group shows that more than half of the 1.1 million families claiming Child Benefit for over-16s in full-time education live on incomes of under £200 a week, countering Labour's claims that Child Benefit is a perk for the rich.

Surviving debt: the PTSD model

Although one of the main causes of debt is poverty, not all the women in debt that I interviewed were living in poverty. Many of them had survived the trauma of being in debt and moved on. But how had being in debt affected them and how had they survived?

Although this is a relatively small study of women in debt, there are generalisations that can be drawn from the similarities I observed. Perhaps the most striking of these centre on the coping mechanisms that many of these women employed as a means of surviving debt.

One model that seems appropriate in view of many of the symptoms exhibited by these women is *post-traumatic stress disorder (PTSD)*. This is defined as the development of symptoms following a psychologically distressing event outside the range of usual human experience.[4] Although it is most often associated with tragedies like natural disasters and accidents it nevertheless reflects quite accurately the trauma of being in debt and may be a useful tool in helping money advice workers to understand better debt's psychological ramifications on women.

The most striking feature that almost all the women I interviewed had in common was the way in which they avoided dealing with their financial difficulties, particularly in the beginning. This *avoidance* as a strategy is one of the key symptoms of PTSD, whereby the trauma is internalised to avoid immediate pain. Many 'escaped' into other activities – Josephine the business woman, for example, threw herself into her work – or spent even more money. Mary the compulsive shopper, for instance, said, 'I thought there was nothing I could do about it, apart from borrowing some more ... or until a miracle happened.'

Most of the women employed this strategy, whether or not they were directly responsible for their debts, until they were eventually forced to face their situations. Mary was given the sack from the bank where she worked after she had been caught stealing. Jennifer had allowed her ex-husband to continue borrowing large sums of money, using the marital home as collateral, even though she knew he was refusing to pay off the arrears on the mortgage, and she and her children lived under the threat of repossession for four years until she finally approached the building society herself. Laura, too, knew her husband had plunged them into debts totalling thousands of pounds with no hope of repaying them, and yet she did nothing about it, colluding in many ways with him by maintaining a conspiracy of silence until he left. Isobel almost lost her house as a student and did not seek help, but was rescued at the eleventh hour by a friend.

These examples may help to explain why people do not get help for themselves when they first get into debt, often leaving it until it is too late or they need professional help to intervene on their behalf. It might also help to explain why most of the women in debt whom I interviewed seemed to find it quite difficult to talk about the feelings they had experienced when they were in debt, as if they were disconnected from them.

Such deep-seated unwillingness to face their problem means that *exposure or events associated with the trauma* – for example the appearance of potentially threatening letters – are experienced by some women in debt solely as causes of intense psychological distress. Mary, the compulsive shopper, said, 'I had about four or five years of torture, realising it was getting too much for me ... by this time I was not paying anything off and I was receiving lots of letters. I used to read them and put them in the bin. After a while I just put them straight in the bin ... it would make me feel sick. I would think, "oh my God, what do I do now?"'

Isobel, the student, said, 'Not answering letters ... has been a big thing for me – not opening my mail and dealing with things at the time because I knew I couldn't pay the bills. But at the same time I knew if I didn't deal with things it'd be far worse. I got into a state where I couldn't open my phone bills because I knew they were going to be too large.'

Psychic numbing is another symptom of PTSD: the traumatised person feels detached or estranged from others who have not been through the same experience. Laura describes feeling different and distant from others when she and her husband were in serious debt and it was still a secret: 'I used to lie to friends and family about what was going on. Gradually I withdrew from my friends. I made excuses not to go out with them as that would also mean spending money.'

Lisa got into debt as a single-parent student. She did not have the support of a family and had no one to reassure her that everything would be OK. In the end, 'I stayed in the house as much as I could and hid from people who knocked on the door. If I saw anyone in the street that I knew I'd ignore them so they wouldn't ask me how I was.'

Another symptom of PTSD is a *lack of a positive self-image*: guilt feelings about what debtors have to do to survive is very much an issue, affecting their self-esteem. Rebecca describes losing her business as devastating: 'So many people suffered as a result of my business collapsing. We didn't manage to pay the advertising agency, the staff were laid off and many of them haven't been able to find a job. The investor lost a staggering amount of money and my husband and I lost the lot ... I see people who worked for me struggling to maintain a basic standard of living. The waste is wicked, the guilt is overwhelming.'

Margaret was in debt because of her heroin addiction. When her parents went on holiday and lent Margaret and her partner their home she sold her father's sword collection and his silver coins and medals. She also got hold of her mother's personal identification number (PIN) and managed to withdraw thousands of pounds over several months undetected; her mother's jewellery was also pawned to buy heroin. 'It felt dreadful. I couldn't understand how I could do that while at the same time I *was* doing it. I couldn't help myself. I couldn't stop myself. I had to shut off the awfulness of it all in the same way I shut off when my son drowned ... the ability to forget it, otherwise I'd just die of pain.'

Elsewhere it is stated that symptoms of *depression and anxiety* are commonly associated with PTSD. These are probably the symptoms most frequently reported by the women in this study. Lisa became extremely depressed and had suicidal feelings when she was struggling to combine studying at college with looking after her two young children on a grossly inadequate student grant. 'I became extremely depressed, although I didn't let it show. I hated everything but I couldn't blame anyone, so in the end I turned it on myself ... I thought seriously about suicide as the best way out and yet I couldn't bear the thought of how it'd affect the children. I knew what it was like having no parents and what it would be like for them if I wasn't there. But I thought perhaps the best way out would be for them to go into a home somewhere and for me to be out of it altogether.'

Mary, the compulsive shopper, describes her behaviour after she had been sacked from work for stealing money. 'I didn't leave the house for ages. I couldn't go out for about six months. I used to sit in front of the breakfast telly in my nightie. Most of my friends dropped me ... it was a real shock.'

Alice's husband walked out after 40 years of marriage and she was left feeling totally devastated and with about £10,000 worth of debts. She is also physically disabled. She attributes her debts to the way in which the divorce was handled. 'I wouldn't be in all this debt now if we had done things differently ... also personally I wouldn't have felt so rejected ... I said to my son recently, "If it were not for the dogs I'd sooner be out of it." It's not only the debts that distress me so much – it's my whole future.'

Drawbacks and limitations of the PTSD model

PTSD is associated with psychiatric illness in connection with a profound shock or loss, usually in the wake of a tragedy. It would therefore be inappropriate to associate women in debt primarily with mental illness.

It places the woman in debt in a potentially passive position and as such may become an 'illness' model. If this happens, it is likely to be counterproductive, particularly since one aim might be to want to empower people in debt by encouraging them to face their problems and take some action, for example participating in getting information they need, asking for help, joining a support group and so on.

Advantages of the PTSD model

- such a model acknowledges the distressing experience of being in debt and the psychological effects it can have on women
- it helps to identify specific psychological factors like avoidance or denial, lack of self-esteem, a sense of failure, depression and anxiety that women in debt might experience
- it could provide the basis of a framework for working with women in debt – either individually or in groups
- it may be useful simply as a source of information to enable money advice workers to respond as sensitively as possible to women in debt
- by associating being in debt with trauma it may help money advice workers better to understand the pressures and expectations on women today and particularly on women in debt

The addiction model

An increasingly popular method of helping people in debt is based on the twelve-step model used in alcohol addiction, where debt – like alcoholism – is regarded as an incurable disease: 'Once an alcoholic, always an alcoholic'. Recovered alcoholics in organisations such as Alcoholics Anonymous always consider themselves alcoholics regardless of how long they have been sober. According to a growing number of organisations, debtors and their uncontrolled spending are like alcoholics and their uncontrolled drinking. Mary the compulsive shopper, who benefited from group therapy, describes herself in the language of a recovering alcoholic when she says she is 'in recovery' and fears that without appropriate help she might return (like an alcoholic) to her old patterns.

Do women in debt have particular issues?

Women's lifestyles have changed dramatically in the last couple of decades and this change may contribute to the vulnerability of women in situations where debt is more likely to occur – especially in their relationships and in the workplace.

New family patterns mean that women are not being supported by men in the way they once were. At least one-third of couples now produce babies outside marriage. Although the Child Support Agency came into force in April 1993 to ensure that both parents have a duty to contribute to the maintenance of their children, it is inefficient, often ineffective, rigid and very slow. Most mothers who are claimants on Income Support are no better off, as any income from child maintenance that exceeds benefit level is deducted. Many are worse off. Laura's story illustrates the failure of the Child Support Agency to secure maintenance payments from her ex-husband, who is earning £60,000 a year while Laura and her two young children are struggling to survive on Income Support.

The recent decline in job security particularly affects women whose working lives are dominated by their position in the family. Low pay, part-time work and women tend to go together. A woman's life cycle affects her earning power. Having children usually means a huge reduction in her income and her working hours and is likely to affect her career prospects and consequently her earning power. In addition, those women who had managed their finances separately had then to negotiate a share of the income with their partners – and often from a position of weakness as a mother who is no longer earning. Several mothers interviewed, like Laura, Margaret and Alice, earned considerably more before they had children; others, like Isobel the university student, who eventually found employment after she graduated, and Josephine the woman in a business partnership, who later became a homoeopath, earned more once their children had left home.

In spite of the 'new woman' image, family responsibilities remain the most important determinant of women's work according to recent findings by the University of Essex, while family considerations have a much smaller impact on men's employment decisions.

Are women's current lifestyles and pressures producing debt-triggering situations to a greater degree? In the UK one in three marriages fails, the highest failure rate in Europe. Women initiate divorce in 73 per cent of cases but are the bigger losers when couples split up: they lose 25 per cent of their income while men gain 16 per cent.[5]

The nature of work has changed and employment is precarious: female unemployment stands at 7 per cent as against 10 per cent for men. There are new types of casual, temporary and contract forms of employment. Jobs are no longer for life, they are not necessarily full-time and different skills may be required at different times in a worker's life: flexibility is required, but this is not accompanied by any social changes that make working easier for women – in particular the provision of adequate child care. Although there has been a recent redistribution of work from men to women, the Conservative government admitted a lack of suitable child care prevented mothers returning to work and this situation has remained virtually unaltered for decades. Nevertheless, women typically work 26 hours a week, making Britain's army of part-timers overwhelmingly female and generally poorly paid. Men work 38 hours. The gender pay gap thus remains twenty years after equality laws were passed. Full-time female workers earned 79 per cent of men's pay in 1994 compared with 71 per cent in 1975, according to the Equal Opportunities Commission.

Women's attitudes to debt

The women in this study carried with them certain beliefs and expectations about their financial situations which seemed to influence how they responded to their financial difficulties. They often related their own experiences to those of their mothers and fathers and recalled childhood memories where their attitudes to money and debt seem to have been formed.

'I can see similarities between James and my dad,' said Jennifer, whose ex-husband always spent almost all his earnings on himself and plunged the family into debt by refusing to keep to any agreements over mortgage repayments so that the family home was eventually repossessed. 'Although my dad is very good with money it is definitely *his* money. My mum has never, ever had any money of her own although she always worked. Her money was used for housekeeping; it was not her own personal money.' Jennifer, like her mother, never kept what she earned for herself. Instead, it too went into the housekeeping – usually to pay off bills.

Mary the compulsive shopper said, 'Looking back ... I realise that no one in my family used to talk about problems. The response to any major catastrophe was: "Let's not talk about it." Problems were never mentioned. When my parents split up ... I realised that they had problems but never knew what they were or why my father left. Mum said she did not want to talk about it. As a child I thought we moved because of my father's job, but looking back I think we were running away from his money problems. Maybe I have reacted to my problems in the same way.'

Josephine almost lost her home, which she put up as collateral with her partner in case their business failed. The business was his idea and she saw herself as going along with it. She was barely paid a wage from it although she worked there full-time for several years. The large debt that the business eventually incurred never really felt as if it was anything to do with her although she was directly affected by the business failing. Although she rather resented the notion that women do not fully understand business it was in fact the case. She had been brought up to believe that 'women really belonged in the home. Women didn't need to work. But I think that throughout the whole of my married life there was always a sense of needing to get out and do something but I couldn't or didn't manage to do that while I was married to my first husband ... my needs always felt as if they were secondary to my partner's – particularly when my children were born. But there was also a degree of relief that at least I didn't have to think about work for a while.'

Women have taken huge strides towards independence from their traditional roles, when they supposedly did not take responsibility for money. In reality, however, they often did, particularly in working-class communities when the man would come home at the end of the week and hand over his wages. His wife would then give him 'pocket money' for his beer, cigarettes and amusements, but would probably not have considered herself entitled to the same. In this sense things have changed profoundly – although this situation still exists, for example, in Emily's story – and many more women work and contribute financially to the household income as a matter of necessity or else manage independently. The stigma of debt, however, especially with the older generation, remains, most probably because of their upbringing.

How should money advice workers respond?

The main criticism of advice agencies voiced by the women in this study was that the information they were given was not always accurate. This is obviously a matter of professionalism, training, honesty, resources and funding. Several said they did not think agencies like Citizens' Advice Bureaux (CABx) would be appropriate to deal with their problems.

The other major criticism was that there did not seem to be an appropriate place for women to go where they felt comfortable with their problems. Again agencies are limited by budgets, but it seems that there is a need for a more consumer-friendly service, particularly for women – one that takes account of the needs of women in debt. It is a sad indictment of our social services that many women do not approach them for help when they desperately need it because of their overriding fear and suspicion that their children will be removed from their care. The need for somewhere to go becomes all the greater for those women who may not have the support of their local community, family or friends.

What can women in debt do to help themselves?

- get professional help as soon as possible
- get support for themselves from friends and/or professionals

- empower themselves by finding out as much as they can about their situation, the options, the likely outcomes and be as actively involved as possible in making any decisions that might affect them

Additional advice from two women in debt:

- 'Be practical,' said Lisa the student. 'It may be possible to go out to work.'
- 'Develop a change of attitude ... debt is a form of powerlessness – like heroin,' said Margaret, who was an addict. 'Change your attitude towards it. Be positive.'

Main facts to emerge

- the most common cause of debt, aside from poverty, seems to be an unexpected change of circumstances, often beyond a person's control: loss of a job, a partner, increase in interest rates or having a baby
- debt and distress usually go hand-in-hand. While the focus of help is to deal with debts, it is also important to recognise the trauma that being in debt may cause and the devastation that people may experience as a result
- several symptoms exhibited by the women who were interviewed were consistent with post-traumatic stress disorder (PTSD), particularly their mechanism for coping with the trauma of being in debt, which was to avoid dealing with their financial difficulties. This avoidance as a strategy continued until they were finally forced to face their situations
- any associations with the debt also had to be avoided to reduce distress, for example the appearance of what they perceived as potentially threatening letters, which were often consigned straight to the wastepaper bin
- other symptoms included depression and anxiety, which they all experienced to some degree; feeling detached and different from others who, unlike them, were not in debt; and feelings of guilt about what they had to do to survive being in debt, for example having to dismiss employees

- the psychological health of the women in this study was affected to a much greater degree than their physical health

- women in debt seem to have particular issues. These include the effects of new family patterns, which may mean that they are no longer being supported by men in the way they once were; also increased job insecurity and the changing – and precarious – nature of employment. These changes are not accompanied by any social changes that make working easier for women, particularly the provision of adequate child care. These issues pose the question of women's current lifestyles possibly triggering situations where debt is more likely to occur

- one cannot ignore the family as a key element in the role of women today – their sexual and reproductive role within it and how this ideology supports low wages and less job security for many women, making them more vulnerable to debt

- a woman's place in the family highlights the double bind that many find themselves in: needing to work and provide adequately for themselves and their children, yet often finding they are unsupported both in the home and in the workplace. This can – and does – influence and shape women's lives and the choices that are open to them

- women have been managing household budgets for generations, although supposedly they did not take responsibility for money. Some of the business women in debt experienced patronising and paternalistic attitudes towards them, by which on the one hand they were not expected to know much about money and yet, at the very least, were simultaneously expected to keep the family – and the business – out of debt. The double standard manifested in this attitude is at its most harsh in the judiciary system, where women unable to pay fines are sent to prison every day – often simply because they are unable to pay their television licences

- managing money efficiently is something we are all expected to be able to do, yet we are not taught how to do this in any formal kind of way

- the expectations on women today – and especially on single parents – are unrealistic given the level of their benefits, which do not take account of unexpected bills like a cooker needing to be repaired or replaced. The Social Fund is supposed to help in such circumstances but fails to do so. As a result women become vulnerable to loan sharks, hire purchase schemes and so on. Benefits continue to be cut and yet women are expected to continue to cope and to stay out of debt

- attitude to debt is important. One CAB worker in Bristol says that in her experience, 'women tend to cope a lot better than men. While both sexes may bury their heads in the sand when it comes to facing their debts, women seem more easily to recognise that it has got to be sorted. Women seem stronger and more coping when it comes to money problems. It's usually the woman who rings up and makes the appointment or drags her partner in off the street to be seen. She tends to do the talking. The men don't seem to take their debt problems as seriously. I've noticed that when the problems get too much for the men they tend to pass it over to the women to deal with. Sometimes they just run away, abandoning their wives, who then have to deal with their debts. I've also noticed that in working-class areas it is the women who handle the money and come into the office whereas in middle-class families they either come in together or they have their own separate accounts. But on the whole it's the women who handle the household budget. When it comes to bigger amounts like mortgage repayments it's usually the man's responsibility. So many women are struggling to cope ... I think it's sad that people don't congratulate them on how well they have done! They don't often see it themselves.'

Debt as a metaphor

The women in this study were forced to look at themselves and their lives in relation to their debts by recounting their experiences and their feelings. They also had to look at how they themselves had participated in creating their own financial difficulties. All of them said that they learnt from the experience and have become better people as a result. Some felt they could cope more confidently with anything they might meet in the future; others said that they had discovered their own inner strength through their experience of being in debt. One described her 'recovery' as due to a change in attitude towards her debts and hence herself, another as a slow process of getting to know herself and feeling OK about herself. Most could not have done this without professional help. For some the experience of surviving debt became a metaphor for their lives. Lisa, the single-parent student who was unable to complete her course, said, 'It was my debt. I had to pay.' Josephine, the woman in a business partnership who almost lost her home, said, 'A lot of my experience was about a struggle to find my own identity and survival.'

Notes

1. 'The Poor Laws', Nick Davies (*Guardian*, 8 February 1996).
2. 'Poor Fall Through Fund's Safety Net', Andy McSmith (*Observer*, 27 November 1994).
3. 'Women Left Out in the Cold Again', Lisa Buckingham (*Guardian*, 27 November 1996).
4. 'Post-traumatic stress disorder', (ref. 309 89, p. 247, DSM 111R), *Diagnostic Manual of Mental Disorders* (American Psychiatric Association, 1987), p. 247.
5. *Changing Households: The British Household Panel Survey 1990–92* (ESRC Centre for Micro-social Change).

2 Separation or divorce

JENNIFER: HOUSE REPOSSESSION

Jennifer is aged 49 and has two children. She has never earned any money that she has been able to call her own. Any money she did earn went straight back into the family – usually to pay off bills. After her divorce a few years ago she allowed her alcoholic ex-husband to continue to borrow large sums of money, using the marital home as collateral. Although he often earned large sums he consistently refused to keep up the mortgage repayments or to keep to any agreements with the building society. As a result, Jennifer and her children have lived under the threat of repossession for the last six years. Jennifer's main concerns during this time were keeping a roof over their heads and the long-term psychological effects of their experience on her children.

Two years ago, on the advice of the local Trading Standards Office (which gives independent consumer advice), Jennifer asked the building society if she could take on sole responsibility for the mortgage – including the arrears – in an interest-only mortgage, but they refused. Apparently they wanted to keep her ex-husband's name on the deeds because they reckoned he was jointly responsible for the arrears – even though he wasn't paying them off. And yet it was because he *defaulted on these payments that the family was threatened with eviction.*

Repossessions in 1996 were running at their highest level for two and a half years, at about 1,000 homes a week. But whose needs are being served with eviction orders – and how often are the wives victims in such cases? Why are the courts not more sympathetic? After all, the actual loan is for considerably longer than the few years that many borrowers like Jennifer and her husband have been in debt to the building society.

The claim made by debt advisers – that a longer period is needed in which people like Jennifer could make more affordable repayments, possibly over the full length of the mortgage – has at last been heard. A recent landmark judgment ruled that home owners could spread their arrears over the full term of the mortgage. This would take account of *people's changing circumstances – for example Jennifer's divorce – so that they could adjust their repayments accordingly. It would also mean that people like Jennifer could make more realistic repayments without living under the threat of repossession or having to endure expensive and traumatic court appearances.*

We began getting into debt about five or six years ago, when I was still with my husband, and I realised we had to do something about it. We'd been living beyond our means. We'd privately educated both our children, which we could not really afford – this was partly because our son was dyslexic and the local authority refused to pay for him to go to a private school to get the necessary help – and we felt we should give our daughter the same opportunity. Also, I thought my husband was capable of earning a lot of money as he is a very, very intelligent person. Now, looking back on it, I can see that his main problem is drink, but I didn't really see it at the time. I felt he drank too much at lunchtime but it was a habit and he liked the socialising – and I had great faith in him. I thought he would sort things out.

I was working in my husband's business. He is a self-employed financial adviser. After a year or so of trying to cut back, I realised our efforts to repay our debts were hardly noticeable. In fact we had always had money problems from the day we met. And I remember, when we went to marriage guidance some years ago, money was a big problem then too. We had lots of arguments about it because we always lived beyond our means. But I was never extravagant. I never spent money on the things I would've liked to do or buy, like clothes or things for the house. I didn't resent it at all. I presumed that one day I would get my reward. Also I'd grown up seeing my mother behave in the same way. She'd always worked part-time and her earnings were never for herself. They were always for the family.

My husband's worst extravagance was his drinking. He had to go to the pub every lunchtime and every evening. I said we couldn't afford it, so the only thing I could do was not to go with him. That way we could save money by not having to pay a baby sitter as well as saving the money that would have been spent on drink for me. I suggested he give me a tenner instead, so I could put the money to better use, but he wouldn't do that. I had no control over the money, even when I eventually went out to work. I worked in an advertising agency and I wasn't earning a great deal, but all that I earned went towards all the standing orders; none of it was for myself. Because he was self-employed and earning only commission he never knew what he would earn. It was never a regular income. If he earned thousands we would spend thousands. He would love to have a nice holiday. He would give me money and tell me to go and buy something nice and I was so pleased to be able to have money I'd go and spend it. And, if there was not any money, he'd carry on spending at the same rate. To give you an idea of how much he spends, he now earns about £1,000 a month. He lives with his mother and pays her nothing at all. He doesn't run a car. He has no outgoings. He's not paying back any of his debts. He very rarely gives any money to me or the kids. Almost all that £1,000 goes on cigarettes and booze, and the occasional meal out. So he's expensive to run and always has been. He spends about £30 a day like this; he has tried to cut it down to £20, but he's never managed it.

I felt he should've been working for the family, not just himself. When I worked for him he didn't pay me anything, and my contribution went towards keeping the family. That's how I think husbands and fathers should work. But James spent everything on himself and we got what was left over. I remember saying to the marriage guidance counsellor about ten years ago – long before we split up – that James's attitude is that whatever he earns each month he takes for himself first, then he'll give me housekeeping and if there's anything left he'll pay the mortgage or the bills; they were always at the bottom of the pile. The counsellor asked him if this was how he handled money and he said, 'Yes.' She tried to suggest that I should handle the money, as I would do it in a very different way, with bills and mortgage coming first, then housekeeping and if there was any left, then *that* was spending money. But James couldn't live like that and he said to me categorically that the first thousand he earns is his, because if he can't have his drink and his cigarettes then life would not be worth living and he would commit suicide. So that's his life, but he'll give me anything that's left over. I can remember one month – the August before last – he got £500 more than the £1,000 he needed and he gave me £300 and £100 to each of the children. He didn't pay off any of the debts. He still owes about £25,000.

I always used to worry terribly about the money. You can't keep on living beyond your means. Then I realised how much it was affecting me and wearing me down. It was making me very, very nervous. I was lacking in confidence. That memory is very vivid.

I felt it was taking away my security. I could no longer rely on my husband and I was always worrying about things. The worry and stress of it was making me nervous. I began to lose faith in my own capabilities. And my faith in him was fading. That was a horrible feeling. I used to liken it to my need to replace James at the helm of a ship, otherwise we would end up on the rocks, but he wouldn't let me take the helm, which is why I opted out of the marriage. It was becoming disastrous.

When I thought about the times we'd got into a really bad hole, like when someone was trying to repossess the car, I realised that James always managed to find a way out. So I thought I must put more faith in him, he's always managed so far, we have never lost the house, he's always got rid of the bailiffs whenever they came; he's always managed to deal with the problem, so I should stop worrying. He can deal with it; he's a financial adviser, that is his business. So I told myself to start trusting him a bit more and to stop getting so uptight about it.

Maybe my attitude in the last couple of years that we were together made things worse. I realised just how much he spent on himself; he was also a member of the golf club and would have golfing holidays, which obviously cost a lot, and I thought, 'This is not fair. If he's spending that much on himself, then I am going to spend that much on *myself*.' He said he thought that was fair enough – that I should have things, that he'd like to give me things. One of the things that he bought for me was a time share in Spain, which we couldn't afford. We actually owned it for two years, which was wonderful. We did have very good holidays. He loved to give me all the things that money could buy, but he lives in a fantasy world as far as money is concerned.

In many ways he was very easy-going as long as it didn't interfere with his drinking. It became more of an effort for me to do the things I wanted to, like going to the theatre, because it often interrupted his drinking time even though he enjoyed the theatre too. The drink was taking over more and more. We did go to get help from an advisory centre for alcoholics and they told him he wasn't an alcoholic! I was there and witnessed everything that he said – like he would have three or four pints at lunchtime and sometimes the same in the evening and sometimes a bit more, like six or seven pints. He's drinking more now than he was when we were together because then he had an evening meal and the children to come back to and I used to deliberately have it ready at seven o'clock to get him out of the pub, where he would've been

Separation or divorce

since 5.30. After supper he'd usually go back to the pub if there was nothing he wanted to see on television. Looking back, I can see how much he's changed, although he's always liked drinking and socialising, but he stopped doing things around the house. He was very good at DIY and made our kitchen units.

But gradually his behaviour changed. He became deceitful. At work I thought he was going out on appointments but later I discovered he was going drinking instead. He nearly always had an 'appointment' about eleven o'clock and would return home for lunch about one o'clock. Then he'd go again after lunch and sometimes be there almost till opening time. I didn't realise how much he was drinking. I also discovered that he was hiding the post from me, in the office and at home. He got up before I did in the morning so he got the post first and he always went to the office in the morning before me. The letters were bills or from bailiffs or the tax man threatening to do things, but in a way I wondered if he wanted me to find out because he would leave them in places like his dressing-gown pocket or once in his dinner-jacket pocket. He actually asked me to take it to the cleaners for him.

Eventually I got him to agree to see an independent financial adviser who would look professionally at our situation – what we owed, what we were worth, everything – to put our cards on the table and ask, 'What do we do now?' And just as were on our way to see this chap, James said, 'By the way, don't mention ... ' some particular loan, I can't remember which one. He never came out with the whole truth to anyone.

The advice that we got was to get out of the house there and then. This was about a year before we split up. We were told to cut our losses on the house, to move into rented accommodation, which would be a lot cheaper for us than repaying our mortgage plus the horrendous arrears, as he'd not paid anything towards it for over a year. I didn't know for quite a while that he hadn't been paying it. They were the sort of letters he was hiding from me. I thought they were paid by standing order. He was very good at covering things up and I was very good at letting him. I didn't want to see what was happening. I wanted a rosy view of life. And I still very much liked and loved him. So I only wanted to see him as I liked to. Things were getting so bad that eventually I got him to go to the doctor. I knew he was not working properly; he was being very, very unreasonable with me. He was referred to a counsellor on the National Health but even then he was not honest with the counsellor as I went a few times myself. So it felt a bit like he was going there to keep me happy.

By July 1990 I was feeling very, very low and told the counsellor, and she said, 'Give me another three to six months and I will sort out your problems.' I told her that I didn't think that I could wait until then, that I was sure I was going to have a nervous breakdown before then, that I couldn't stand how things were at home any longer. My husband wouldn't communicate anything to me and when he did it was all lies. I didn't think I could cope any more. She suggested that I find out what the situation would be if we did split up.

I went to see a solicitor. He told me that normally any assets are split between husband and wife, but since there weren't any assets and an awful lot of debts they would be split between us. That really frightened me. He said they were joint debts, like school fees, even though they were in his name. I've since found out that this advice was wrong, along with other advice that he gave me. I didn't want James to know that I'd been to a solicitor so I had to ask questions subtly. But he found out anyway. I certainly didn't want to divorce my husband and I thought he might get a bit frightened if he knew I'd seen a solicitor. But I needed to know where I stood.

During the next few months things were very much better. James started working much harder and was earning £3,000 to £4,000 a month most of the time. But he was still not being totally honest and I was finding that very difficult. The counsellor at that time suggested that I should try and provide a peaceful, loving home for James and not to upset him in any way by asking questions and so on. But she also acknowledged that I needed my questions answered. So there was to be one evening a week set aside so we could discuss things. This lasted about two or three weeks and then he just didn't come home on those nights. I found it so frustrating. If we weren't going to talk about anything we weren't going to get anywhere. So one evening when he came home late for supper I just said very calmly to him and the children that he'd be leaving us as there was no way we could carry on as we were. Then, quite calmly, he said, 'Can I have my supper first?' and I said he could but that he had to pack up after that, which he did. There was no argument when I asked him to go. He knew exactly how badly everything was affecting me.

At the time I thought that his way of coping with it was by not talking about it. So I thought he needed the space and that this

Separation or divorce

was very much a temporary thing. He returned home a few weeks later for Christmas and I wondered whether he would leave afterwards. He had slotted in very easily to a bachelor lifestyle and announced on the first night back, just as I was cooking dinner, that he was off to the pub. I know I hadn't been part of his life for a few weeks, but I was very hurt that he hadn't thought to ask me to go with him. After two weeks he packed his bags and left again, although I heard he was often seen crying in the pub about how much he missed me. Everyone thought what a bitch I was and that I'd chucked him out because we had run out of money and that I'd always spent it all. But what would they have seen if they'd looked in my wardrobe or around the house?

It was a very difficult time for me. I'd lost my husband and my job and I didn't really have my friends as they drank in the same pub as James and obviously I couldn't go there any more. When people did see me out and about and in other pubs I appeared to be quite happy, whereas James was often quite unhappy. I knew they thought, 'Poor James. He's got nowhere to live.' He had left me the house and the car and wasn't I lucky? It was very hurtful for a while and at times I felt quite resentful, especially when I was with our old friends who seemed quite happy together. They had a nice house, nice holidays. I would think, 'How come it's me who's married the man with the problems?' In some ways it made me feel that I had to try harder. Also James was never nasty. It was difficult to be angry with him. Perhaps in some ways that made it harder for me to resent him and what he was doing. Perhaps the pressure of not having money made him drink more. If there had been enough money everything would've been fine. I would've put up with things because he's a nice person, the father of our children. We had had good times together and we get on so well. Looking back though, I think that in some ways I was quite lucky it got so bad as I had an excuse to end it. I would've found it very difficult to end it myself although I was not very fulfilled, I most probably would've stayed with him. I don't believe in divorce unless there is a very good reason ... 'for richer, for poorer'. That didn't help me as I've lived for a long time with the guilt of ending the marriage. I still feel that guilt although I know it was James's behaviour that brought it to an end. Also it was seen by everyone else as my ending it because I asked him to leave.

Eventually I decided that I had to pull myself together so I got on a computer course to get myself back into work. When I applied, someone noticed that I hadn't declared my marital status. I said I was unsure about what it was and was told that as he wasn't paying me any money I should be entitled to Income Support from Social Security. Within a few days somebody came to visit me and from then on I was getting something like £250 a week! It was wonderful! This was for the mortgage, two children who were still in full-time education and for me as a single parent. My son was attending a college of further education and managed to get a grant of £1,000 per year, so that helped a lot and my daughter was still at school. They kindly waived her fees. I was worried they would throw her out as we were already in arrears with the fees, but they allowed her to stay on for her final year provided the arrears were paid off, as they thought it was in her best interest. So that was wonderful. All in all I felt reasonably well off. When James found out I was on Income Support he agreed to pay £200 per month off the arrears, especially those on the mortgage, which at that time amounted to about £5,000.

Everything went well for a while until about mid-1993, when I got a letter from the building society regarding the mortgage. Prior to this there had been a possession order on our house, but provided James kept to the arrangement of paying £200 per month off the arrears they would not enforce the order. But James hadn't stuck to the agreement. The letter was giving me 28 days' notice to vacate the property. There'd been no warning from them before that. None at all. It was horrendous! I didn't even cry, I was so stunned and numb. My son was at home and we both wandered round the house like zombies, unable to believe we were going to lose the house. In fact my son was working in his uncle's pub and was actually watching his father down all these pints of beer but not pay the £200 a month to keep us in our house. As a result my son lost a lot of respect for his father.

I knew James was paying off the arrears occasionally, but I thought he kept in touch with them. This was another thing that we'd always disagreed about – I thought you should let people know when you were unable to make a payment or at least to pay part of the debt. But James would never, ever do that. He'd go for months without notifying anyone that he was unable to pay, then they'd eventually contact him and he'd say, 'Here's £300' or whatever with a promise to keep up the rest of the payments, but he never did. He'd always manage to get round them somehow and to keep it all going, which always amazed me.

I think he felt that he could only pay his debts if the money was spare money. He didn't get so embarrassed that he'd pay the money or feel he ought to pay. He belonged to the same club as our local mechanic who always used to repair our car. He owed him quite a bit of money and of course would see him socially at the club. But instead of paying him, he simply changed garages. I don't understand his attitude, but perhaps it has got something to do with being very intelligent – that if you are intelligent you are supposed to make money. He was privately educated and his mother had money. She paid for his education and she always had the power to override any decision her husband might make when it involved money. His brother is worth a lot of money but he's worked very hard for it. They are so unalike. James feels he's worked hard when he's been in the office from 10 till 12.30 and from 2 until 5.30.

After getting this letter I went to the council's local Trading Standards Office. They give independent advice to consumers on a whole range of financial matters. It was then that I found out that James should never have been made responsible for the arrears because he was not living under the same roof, and yet he *was* made responsible for the repayments. Even with the Trading Standards Office trying to sort out everything for me with the Social Security and what should have been paid and why the arrears were so huge, it took almost a year to try and sort things out. That's when Social Security made a payment to my building society of £1,000 because they had been under-paying. There had been a mix-up between the building society and Social Security regarding information on their forms. We had a mortgage and a £5,000 loan and the interest on the loan should've been paid by Social Security, but it wasn't paid, and the interest on the arrears should've been paid by me from my benefit apparently. This should've been happening since January 1991 when I first received Income Support – up until July 1993. When we separated the arrears were £5,000 and they are now £14,000. I'd been told that while the Trading Standards Office was in touch with the building society from July 1993 to February 1994 that the arrears would not increase. At the time they stood at around £8,000. The Trading Standards Office said it was the worst case they had ever come across.

Lately it has all come up again and I've had another letter from the building society saying there is a shortfall on the payment between what Social Security pay and what the monthly payment should be. This is £96.47 per month and has to be paid from October 1994. I can't understand why none of this came up before when the building society and the Trading Standards Office were in touch. Unfortunately the person who dealt with my case at the Trading Standards Office has left and so has the person at the building society, so I'm finding it really difficult at the moment to get any help from anybody and I'm wondering just where I can go now. Meanwhile James has been served with bankruptcy papers and the house is in joint names. The building society wouldn't release it into my name because they say that James is responsible for the arrears. My solicitor had been trying to get the house put in my name, but has only managed to get the equity of the house (of which there is none) in my name. But since we separated, several people that he owes money to have put charging orders on the house, which means those debts will have to be paid. Apparently they could even prevent the house from being sold if they felt they weren't going to get their money. Also they don't want the house put in my name as it would affect them getting their money back. So it's getting very complicated with the bankruptcy as well as the threat of the possession order. I feel like chucking the keys back at the building society and renting a bed-sit. But I'm told it's good to hang on to property and it does feel right to hang on and I'm hoping that one day there'll be some equity. But that seems like such a long way off, especially with arrears of £14,000. But at least it is a roof over our heads. Although it's costing £600 a month it would probably cost that much to rent somewhere for all of us. That does not include the arrears of £200 a month. That's why I can't go out to work. I couldn't earn that sort of money after tax!

The reason the Trading Standards Office said my case was the worst they had ever come across was because it was so complicated: the mortgage, the loan, the arrears and the fact that it took so long to sort out as well as all the forms presumably being filled in incorrectly. But the other thing that's now come up is that I've discovered that the endowment policy was changed to a repayment policy back in April 1990 by the building society because we got into arrears. James and I were still together then, so there was probably a letter that I didn't see. Also there were two endowment policies which would've been worth something and they were cashed in and went towards paying off the arrears. I suppose the building society did this and notified James. I

Separation or divorce

don't know. The policies were in his name, not in joint names like the house.

It's left me feeling really helpless. I've always had the attitude that you can do something about a problem – work a bit harder or whatever – but I seem to be in such a helpless situation not only because I can't help myself financially but also because everything seems to go wrong all the time. I can't believe what's happened now, like the repayment mortgage. There were three organisations communicating about us: the building society, the Social Security and the Trading Standards Office. How could it never have come up all those months? But what's upsetting is that, when all this came to light, the Trading Standards Office suggested that I quickly take out an endowment policy before the building society found out, as apparently I needed one to enable me to continue with the mortgage, which had to include interest payments. I did this and have been paying over £100 a month on it and now I find out that I didn't need it because the mortgage had already been converted to a repayment mortgage – which includes interest as well as capital repayments – and my husband hadn't told me! I have been paying it for seven months. If you stop paying after seven months you get nothing back but if you keep it going for a year you get £1,000 back. So I'm having to borrow £100 a month to pay it off.

I've kept an awful lot from the children and when I do try and talk about it my son feels it's parents' problems, which I agree with up to a point, but at 21 I feel he should be willing to share them. He's willing to share in that he realises he has to pull his weight financially – more than most kids his age – but I don't think it has done him any harm. He always has to pay me when he's living at home whether he's working or not, and that includes the holidays, and he has to replace the petrol in my car if he uses it. I feel sorry for them at times, especially when we do things like going round the supermarket. I'd like to be able to buy them little things like deodorant or shampoo, but I can't. It's strictly household stuff. They have to buy those things themselves. But they know that I've done everything I possibly can financially and in other ways, but I do worry about how they feel about their dad and how it will affect them. Obviously they love him, but for them not to respect their father and to resent how he lives and to disapprove of him is worrying in terms of how it might affect them in the long term, particularly for my daughter because they say that girls marry their dads. What sort of man will she marry? I can see now similarities between James and my dad, although my dad is very good with money but it's definitely *his* money. My mum has never, ever had any money of her own although she always worked. Her money was used for housekeeping; it was not her own personal money.

I've never had my own money. Before I went out to work I used to earn money at home. We had live-in students and I also did bookkeeping from home, but the money from that was never considered my money. It was for housekeeping. Actually I took great delight in changing the names on all the bills after James left, like the gas and so on, so they were now in my name only. I enjoyed that; even though they were bills – they were *mine*. In spite of getting into debt on Barclaycard since we split up, I'm still quite proud of how I have managed on so little money. I've had some help from my family, but that gets harder as time goes on. They were willing to help in the early years but they can't go on doing that. And that's what gets more worrying for me: the fact that it's an ongoing thing. What I find very, very frightening is being on my own in old age. I've got no pension or anything, which is another reason why I want to hang on to the house. Although there are another eighteen years to go – and I would be 67 – until I can afford to do something on my own and the children are no longer a responsibility, I'm stuck.

I do think there should be somewhere for people in my situation to go where there is more specialised help available. I've been to the Citizens' Advice Bureau several times with a pile of bills and they were no help whatsoever. Also, it would've helped to have been put in touch with a solicitor who knew about entitlements and Social Security (which I had originally asked for). In my experience people do not seem to know. The building society adamantly told me that my loan could not be paid by Social Security. Eventually they discovered that the Social Security will pay because it is a loan secured against the house and it might mean that otherwise you lose the house. I wish I'd been told that I could've got financial help from Social Security for essential repairs on the house. Instead, I've had to borrow money to have the roof mended. Also I didn't know other people on Income Support. I didn't have anyone I could go to who knew the system, things like places that sell good-quality household items very cheaply to people on Income Support. I've often thought I should write something on information that people ought to have when they get into debt. Also their entitlements. I didn't know I was

Separation or divorce

eligible for Income Support. I wouldn't have known that the children were entitled to a grant. They found out at college. Independent advice is really important. I've found the Social Security to be very inefficient. I often used to get several letters a day from them – maybe four or five – telling me what I was entitled to. In the end I gave up reading them. I would get different amounts every week although my circumstances never changed. You have to know all the right questions to ask and often you don't. It's all about getting the proper help.

Since our interview Jennifer and her children have lost their home. The court granted a possession order after her building society won the case on appeal on the grounds that Jennifer's repayment agreement made in a previous court case a few months earlier was so low – as she is a claimant – that it would have taken 98 years for her to pay it back.

Her children are now students and have found accommodation elsewhere. Jennifer has found a one-bedroom flat locally. She is left feeling a mixture of relief and anger – directed mainly at the building society for refusing to allow her to take over the mortgage on an interest-only basis when she approached them two years ago – thereby avoiding this whole situation. Instead, they insisted that her ex-husband was responsible for the debts – even though he was not paying them off. Yet it was because he had defaulted on these payments that the family's home was repossessed.

For further details see Chapter 9. Mortgage repayments and house repossession.

LAURA: DIVORCE AND FAILURE TO SECURE CHILD MAINTENANCE PAYMENTS

This story highlights the emotional difficulties for a wife whose husband's excessive spending ended in bankruptcy. While he was out spending far in excess of his earnings, she was at home looking after their two young children and worrying about the debts. But although she worried, she thought things would get better and that he would change; she colluded with him to keep it a secret from their family and friends; although she loathed his spending, in some ways she admits she perpetuated it. It was the bond that held them together until she told him that she was no longer prepared to go on living in debt.

Three years after their separation Laura is still very much affected by his debts, but in a different way. He has simply ignored the Child Support Agency and continues to refuse to make any payments whatsoever towards the maintenance of his children. Laura's solicitor is trying to sue the CSA. In the meantime Laura lives on Income Support and her ex-husband is earning in excess of £60,000 a year.

I grew up in a family where I was taught how to manage money. Before I got married I had my own flat, my own car, and I had independent savings. All that changed as soon as I walked down the aisle. Looking back I blame my ex-husband for a lot of it because he is a person who lives for today. He believed in credit. If he wanted something he would get credit and buy it. So my lifestyle changed completely to my having to do without so that he could have what he wanted. It just became a habit. I did without. I bought second-hand things for the children, my parents subsidised me and he went out and spent money on credit. He even bought a Porsche on credit. He went on skiing holidays with his friends and without me and the children. So it is tied in not only with debt but with his whole attitude and sense of responsibility.

I didn't mind doing without to begin with – it felt OK. Jeremy was the breadwinner and I was very much in love with him: 'Love is blind.' I didn't see any of the warning signs. Common sense went out of the window. I rationalised it to myself: he was important at work, he needed to spend huge amounts on the most expensive clothes and shoes. I was subservient. I was almost grateful to be married to such a successful, wonderful person. I was secondary and so were the children, and I accepted that. We were glad to be supportive; we were proud to be associated with him.

I don't think it ever crossed Jeremy's mind that I was having to do without. If there was money in the bank he assumed that it could be spent on anything. I talked to him lots of times about it and his response would be to cut up his credit cards. But then he would go and get another one. Sometimes he would tell me about it and justify why he had done it. Like a lot of wives and partners, I trusted him and that included trusting him with my money. I loved him. Somehow I allowed it to happen by pretending it was not happening.

I never told my parents about what was going on. Lots of people would ask where Jeremy got the money and I would say he was earning it. Like a lot of women I just carried the whole thing. Once you have children you are so determined to make everything look OK to the outside world that you sacrifice your individuality. The thing that made it very traumatic was that at no point did Jeremy ever say that he wanted to change – that his marriage was more important, or his children.

At the time I naïvely thought things would get better, that things would come right. I never thought of seeing a counsellor about our financial situation. Whenever I went for any therapy or acupuncture, it was always me taking in my problems. It felt almost like I had brought it upon myself.

I remember seeing the Porsche in the driveway and thinking, 'I hate it!' I didn't want to drive it. Jeremy couldn't believe that I was not over the moon about it. Then he would turn up with something else and I would always put a dampener on it. That happened all the time. He would bring home something new and I'd be negative about it, saying that we couldn't afford it. I think that was one of the main reasons that we split up. I felt totally separate from him. It was as if we had nothing in common. It seemed as if he had no respect for me and I had none for him.

I felt that I was trying to make the marriage work, but that he had pulled out completely. He didn't want any responsibility. He became emotionally absent. He wanted a family like an accessory. His attitude to life was that money can buy everything – it can impress people, enable him to have friends. My father had been very careful with money and it was as if the rebellious side had come out in me. Every time my parents turned up we would have a new stereo, a new television, loads of expensive, new things. On the one hand I hated the things and yet I liked them too. It was the emotional cost of having all this stuff around me and yet going to bed and crying about it. My husband would not sit down and talk to me about it. He still believes that the way he lives is right.

One of the worst things is that I used to lie to friends and family about what was going on. I would cover up for Jeremy, saying that he had got a bonus and not that it was on credit and that we were thousands and thousands of pounds in debt. Gradually I withdrew from my friends. I made excuses not to go out as that would also mean spending money. I felt guilty going on holiday or eating out – or even buying a pair of knickers! I was being too loyal. Also I still had this stupid idea that things would get better and that he would change. At the time it seemed the right thing to do although it made me feel sick, especially with my parents subsidising us whenever they saw us. My mum would buy the kids shoes and make clothes for them. She knew we were hard up but she didn't know how hard up we were or why. I kept on lying to cover up. In fact I became as bad as Jeremy. It affected every aspect of our lives together – our sex lives, everything. You can't be close to somebody who is not treating you fairly. I think he had affairs, so his money was going to other women as well. Everywhere except the family.

Looking back I should have put my foot down earlier, but it was the 1980s – the time of excess. Perhaps I was too frightened to say 'stop' or 'no' or else I kept up this pretence that it would get better. I minimised what was happening, but the effects of doing that hurt me terribly. It made me feel very unattractive, of no value. I was overweight from having had two children within a year of each other. So I pushed all my feelings down inside myself. I had one close confidante, my friend next door. I used to moan to her but as a lot of my girlfriends seemed to be in similar types of marriages – the husband working all hours and socialising with people other than their wives – it became acceptable. I felt left out and I was 'not much fun', according to Jeremy. I had become 'serious and boring' since having children. So he chose to go out drinking with men and women from the office, would stay 'late' at work rather than come home and bath his boys. I felt like I had been demoted from the most important person in his life to no one special, but I put on a brave face and prayed. I didn't feel as if I had any power or any tools to bargain with – except perhaps sex, but that rarely worked – it still felt as if it was my problem.

It was a vicious circle: things began to deteriorate, he was working long hours, I was no fun to be with, he came home less and less often and the children were caught up in the middle of it. I felt totally unsupported as a wife and mother from the outset. It was like being a single parent. Jeremy would only turn up when his friends and family were visiting. He became totally indifferent to me; he didn't even criticise what I was doing with the boys. He just pulled out. I felt very isolated and alone. I felt emotionally abused. If it had been visible – if he had had a drugs problem or gambled – I would have had lots of sympathy. But it was invisible – a wearing-down process. At the time I didn't even realise it was going on.

Separation or divorce 37

In many ways I kept it all going. The worse it became – the debts and his emotional abuse – the more determined I was to make it look all right to the outside world and the more he took advantage of it. He depended on me being able to cope, to do without, and not to moan about it. To be loyal. I was in a 'no-win' situation. Every few months I would have a huge outburst, cry, shout, ask him for help, beg for some attention. He would nod, never raise his voice and agree to everything. I remember once he promised to cut down on the spending and not long afterwards he justified spending £200 taking a 'client' out for a meal.

I think that money plays a major part in the way that we show that we care for each other so that when a husband goes out to work to pay the joint mortgage it's a way of showing his love. Jeremy would pay the mortgage, but we were permanently in debt and there was no way I could ever have anything new. He would have a gold card, which automatically allowed him to have a £10,000 overdraft. He was attracted to anyone who offered finance. He would keep on changing our mortgage every year to try to get a better deal, or so he could remortgage. We had huge debts. We had the Porsche, which he bought on credit for £25,000 and sold for £12,000. So we lost over £10,000 cash on a whim! He never said he was sorry. I never really knew where I was with him. I realised after we separated that he is a compulsive liar. He probably lied to me from the outset. Money was the only tangible 'proof' that showed me he didn't care for us as the bank account was always empty. I couldn't face up to that at the time, so I ignored my own feelings and needs.

I carried all this around with me. It was in direct contrast to my childhood, where my father always ensured that his wife and children never went without, so Jeremy's attitude towards me made me – and the children – feel as if we didn't matter; that we weren't important to him. It felt like we didn't count. He would only buy the children stupid, flashy things that they didn't need – like an electric car or a huge climbing frame.

I'm 38 and he's 34, but he's like a 12-year-old. His whole attitude to debt was that it didn't matter. It just didn't matter. I was paranoid about being in debt. I didn't have debt collectors knocking at the door. It was all about juggling the debts and borrowing from one to pay off another. And all the anxiety and stress that goes with that. I know I still need to let go of it all. That's why I have taken up meditation.

At the time I felt as if I had nobody on my side. I was too busy covering up and putting my energy into that. Perhaps as women we are too flexible sometimes and we adapt too easily; we take on all the family's problems. We put on a brave face. We feel responsible. Women often go without or spend a lot of their time economising because of their children's needs. Is it genetic or is it due to social conditioning? I remember going to see a healer for help. The attitude was: 'You are responsible for your life. You need to change it.' But at that point I was still in the 'things will get better syndrome'. I wasn't aware of debt counsellors around at that time, not like today. Also the problem was that Jeremy held the purse strings, so my seeing a counsellor without my husband seemed to be a bit pointless. The other person isn't going to change unless they really want to. In the meantime I would wear my sister-in-law's cast-offs that she gave away. I think his family had some idea of what was going on. They thought he was a bit of a jack-the-lad. But, like me, they never thought he could be so awful. They are very nice to him. No one ever reprimands him for his spending except me, and he never took me seriously. So all the signals he gets from everyone suggest to him that he can do as he likes.

We stayed together for about five years, but our relationship started going downhill after our second child was born. Our boys are 7 and 8 now. We split up in April 1993 after I asked him whether or not he wanted to stay married. I knew he was about to be declared bankrupt and I even offered to support him! But he made it clear that he was seeing other women and having a good time as a 'single' man. So there was no real discussion about it. He decided he didn't want to be married and wasn't cut out to be a husband or a father. I think he was bored. I felt betrayed and let down. Conned and hurt.

He still owes my parents money. He owes my dad £6,000, and yet he has not paid him back although he is earning a fortune. My mother even paid for his vasectomy. It is farcical! He couldn't afford the £89 at the time to have it and we were afraid of having any more children. I think my parents have some idea about his situation, but we've never really discussed it.

I find it incredible that he can still get credit even though he is bankrupt! At the moment he's got an American Express card. It's as if what he has done and how he has spent his money counts for nothing. His own family let him pay the £240 for lunch for the six of them recently and not one of them asked, 'Shouldn't this money be going to your wife and children?'

His family is very supportive towards me but they don't make much of an effort to keep in touch with the boys and rarely visit, especially now that we have moved further away. They're all very embarrassed about what has happened but they don't want to talk to him about it. It's as if they believe that if they don't talk about it, it'll all go away. Jeremy's new girlfriend has been accepted by his family. I'm going to write to them saying it's up to them as to the sort of relationship they have with the children, but that it's their responsibility to make contact with them. I'm not going to continue to drive hundreds of miles so that they can see them.

Jeremy's father walked out on his mother when he was seven and he never paid any maintenance. There were four children and according to Jeremy he fended for himself. He says he has forgiven his father, but makes no effort to see him and certainly has no relationship with him. He's not into relationships. Not even with his own kids. He sees them as my responsibility, just as he and his siblings had been his mother's.

I'm still very much affected by him and the financial problems that we had, even though we've been separated for almost three years. We're not divorced yet because we're unable to sort out a financial settlement until the bankruptcy is sorted out. The Bankruptcy Order lasts for three years. So Jeremy still holds the power.

I asked him what he would've done if I'd brought all this to a head earlier by saying that I wasn't prepared to go on living in debt. He said he would've left a lot earlier. Deep down I knew that. So in a sense I kept the whole thing going. I let Jeremy walk all over us, I let him spend, I signed credit agreements. I completely lost my self-respect. I functioned on 'autopilot'. Except for the occasional outburst I maintained a false sense of stability. I lost all sense of direction – of right and wrong. I simply focused on maintaining the status quo. I desperately wanted someone else to sort it all out or for Jeremy to change: to stop spending and to deal with all the debts.

Looking back I think I felt that a lot of our problems at the time were my fault. I was boring – I had become serious, obsessed with our financial security. I was almost waiting for everything to fall to pieces. I felt that I'd chosen the wrong man, that I'd failed. I didn't know what the rules were but it felt like I had somehow broken them. I'd driven Jeremy to spending, to staying out. I'd pushed him away. It was only by pretending that nothing was going wrong, by trying to be an exciting wife and not moaning about money – in fact totally suppressing my whole self – that there was a chance that we could survive.

I covered up for Jeremy because I thought his spending was a phase – that things would get better. That was why I told friends that he'd had a bonus to buy the stereo instead of a huge overdraft. They'd never have to know as we would eventually pay it off. I couldn't tell the truth because if I did and they discovered what Jeremy was really like they'd pity me. Then I'd have to face up to the person I had really married: a selfish, arrogant bastard who put his own needs before his family's. It was more important to have a 'happy ending' than to hold on to my own beliefs, even though I made myself dreadfully unhappy in the process. I couldn't admit that my marriage was a failure. I had a duty to my children to keep us all together. If I confronted him he would've either walked out or withdrawn even further. I kept myself busy and held everything in. I felt I'd created this mess so I had to pay for it in some way.

Money – and all the debts – meant nothing to Jeremy. It didn't bring him happiness. He was never content or satisfied, even when he had the Porsche, the motorbike, the marine jet etc. etc. It was like he was searching for fulfilment and thought he could buy it with a credit card. He took no responsibility for the debts he had created. It was like he didn't believe they existed. Even when he was made bankrupt he blamed it on everyone else. He walked out shortly afterwards and left me to cope with the mess – including having to apply for Housing Benefit and Social Security as well as having to tell his family about our financial situation.

I am amazed that physically I am fine. I haven't been ill in spite of all that has been going on. I'm very stressed, irritable, angry, lots of emotional stuff – especially revenge! If something happened to Jeremy, like he lost his job, it would seem like natural justice because of the way he has behaved. He has had hundreds of thousands of pounds pass through his fingers and he has filtered this into his life, his way of living and never once said I should have any.

The Child Support Agency defies belief. I know some fathers that are being grossly overcharged and yet someone like Jeremy, who has been earning huge amounts of money for the last three years, is paying nothing. I've cost this country thousands. My Housing Benefit alone was nearly a thousand pounds a month when we lived in London and they are quite prepared to pay me that instead of saying, 'Hang on! Why isn't her ex-husband paying some of this?' I thought this was the reason the Child Support Agency was set up, but I don't hear of any 'good' stories. I do know that couples are not notifying the agency, not getting involved with it at all, but making their own independent financial arrangements. I have written to the CSA loads of times. My solicitor has threatened them with either contacting an MP or a newspaper.

The children understand that the reason we split up is mainly because of money problems. They haven't had everything I would like to have given them and I have to watch my younger son as he seems to have the same attitude to money as Jeremy. I want them to grow up respecting money, but not letting it control them. I am living on £75 a week. Jeremy will send money for the boys but it's for luxury things like their football lessons, not the water rates. It's as if he's saying that the state can pay. A lot of men seem to think like that. Why should they pay for their families? Why should they pay the CSA when they think it doesn't go straight to their families? We would get it anyway from the state – whether or not they pay. They have no conscience about earning huge amounts of money but letting the tax payer support their children.

Living the way I have done since we married has knocked the stuffing out of me. I've forgotten who I am, where I'm going. I would rather be enjoying myself than dealing with all this emotional shit around Jeremy. I'm still dealing with the effect he's had on me and it's still coming out. I'm working very hard on it but I would like to be spending more time being happy – doing joyful things. Having fun. I would like to be independent of him so I could tell him to get lost.

I think as women we undersell ourselves, especially in relationships where the man is earning the money. It's as if we lose all our rights, our credibility, our opinions, our status. I would never have another relationship like that. I still have a lot of stuff to sort out. I wish I could get rid of him. Cut him out.

If I met a woman in a similar position to me, I'd advise her to have a certain amount from his pay put into a separate bank account for security. At the time I didn't believe in having a separate account. I didn't see the need. But looking back I wish I'd done that. I wish I'd said that I needed a certain amount for housekeeping so that it would've meant him having the allowance – not me. Any time I did something like that we would be forced to draw on it in order to pay the mortgage when things got tight. So I ended up paying for it anyway.

When I look back I realise I was very angry at the time, but I didn't recognise it. I suppressed my feelings totally and I consciously chose not to have any. I didn't want to face the fact that money was more important to Jeremy than his own family. Meanwhile the scale of debt – *his* debt – ate away at me. My anger, not only at his treatment of me and the boys but at his total disregard for our financial security, has surfaced only relatively recently. And the fact that he hasn't changed in his attitude to the boys and money generates more anger. I'm also angry with myself for letting it happen – for allowing myself to be taken in by him. I don't want him to be happy. I want him to face the consequences of his actions. I want him to cry and be hurt – to despair.

I also feel I've lost the 'softer' side of me because my life was focused for such a long time on debt, money and financial insecurity. I seem to have lost a 'happy-go-lucky' part of me. I had to be serious for both of us. I'm still very money-conscious and can't spend it easily on myself. I find it hard to pamper myself and to let go of its power.

Women are usually the ones who get dumped and left with the children. We have not moved on; it's still not a financial option for most women to bring up children independently. A lot of men seem to look to the state to provide for their families. They may like the idea of having children – and want to be friends with them when they are older – but often they don't want the hassle or responsibility. They want to stay little boys, and when we marry them we should keep this in mind and give them pocket money – not all their salary – they can't handle it.

Jeremy has recently moved to the Far East, which is outside English jurisprudence. Consequently the Child Support Agency has become even more impotent. Laura says that her husband has made an offer to pay £1,000 per month for child maintenance. But she does not believe one word of it.

For further details see Chapter 12. Separation and divorce.

EMILY: A 'BATTERED' WIFE BECOMES INDEPENDENT

Emily was once a 'battered' wife with absolutely no control over her finances, including child benefit. She felt she had no right to anything. Her husband spent almost every penny that came into the house on alcohol. He even stole money from her purse. She discovered at the eleventh hour that the family was about to be evicted because he had not paid the rent.

With appropriate help she secured her own tenancy with the local authority and had everything transferred into her name. The sense of independence from managing her own finances and the self-esteem that was unleashed by this step has had a profound effect on her life and her relationships – especially her relationship with her husband. She now has a completely different way of seeing and doing things.

The reason we got into debt was that my husband was an alcoholic. He was unemployed and we used to get his unemployment benefit once a fortnight. He was supposed to pay the rent and gas and electric out of that but he didn't. I found out he was also backing horses with it. The giro was in his name. The benefit agency wouldn't put it in my name because he was the one who was unemployed. We had three children at the time – two by my first marriage. They were aged about 12, 7 and 2. I was 40 and this all happened about ten years ago.

Before we got married he was fine. So was I. I had been managing my own money quite well since I split up with my previous husband, about a year before I met Patrick. But as soon as we got married it all changed. He spent all our income on drink and started taking money out of my purse as well. One day I opened a letter from the council. It was an eviction order. Until then I didn't realise that we were in serious debt. He handled all the money. He always used to get up before me and open the mail. Then I discovered the electricity was about to be cut off because the bills had not been paid, and it was the same with the gas.

My main reaction was to worry about what was going to happen to me and the children. I thought that I might lose them – that social services might take them away because we had nowhere to live. Also their dad wanted custody. I think his way of getting back at me was through the children. He didn't pay anything towards their keep and it would've been a waste of time asking him. I had taken it to court to try and get money out of him, but I got nowhere. I wouldn't have benefited anyway because the money would have been deducted from my benefit. So I gave up trying to get maintenance.

I went to the council straight away and they told me to go to Social Security. I was able to claim for myself and the three children in my own right. I was able to pay the rent after that as well as something each week towards the arrears. I also had the gas and electricity transferred into my name. I became responsible for everything from that moment on, but not for the debts when they were in my husband's sole name. We were still living together and he was then claiming only for himself.

My husband had a real problem with drink. He couldn't be without it. He couldn't even get up in the morning without first having a drink. He was brought up with drink around him. It had always been part of his life. I remember the doctor telling us that some people are born alcoholics. That was what it felt like. He was also heavily addicted to cigarettes. He smoked about 60 a day as well as loose tobacco.

Although I paid the bills I didn't really feel that I was in charge of the purse strings. I had to hide my money from Patrick otherwise he would take it and spend it on drink. It affected our relationship a lot. We had a lot of rows, especially about money.

I decided that I couldn't take it any more. It was not only because we had very little money to live on; it was also his violence towards me. And mental cruelty. He started knocking me around as soon as we got married. Once he broke my arm. I also have scars on my inside lower lip where my teeth got pushed through when he attacked me. I had lots of black eyes and bruises. I still have problems with my eyes as a result of him hitting me. I finally went to court and got an injunction to get him out. There was a power of arrest attached to it should I need to contact the police.

I was too ashamed to tell anyone about what was going on. I couldn't bring myself to talk about how he had squandered our money on drink and gambled away the rest. The children and I were having to live on about £10 a week. This was about fifteen years ago. I was very skinny then. Fortunately the kids had free school meals. I made sure they had breakfast before they went. I used to make meals out of baked beans and chips and sausages. I tended to eat what was left over. You have got to put the kids first. My oldest child knew what was going on and that I got

Separation or divorce

knocked about. He never touched them, though he went for my daughter once or twice because she was mouthy to him. I used to have to tell her to keep her mouth shut. But sometimes she would have a go at him as soon as he walked in and then I'd have to stop it – get in between them. I sometimes got hit then.

It was hard not having any control over anything – especially the finances. I had been managing quite well when I was on my own with my two children. It was quite easy. I knew where I was with my money. I would put so much by each week for gas and electric and so on. That lasted for about a year or so until I met Patrick. And then suddenly I had no control over anything. As soon as we got married he had everything changed into his name. The only income I had was the Child Benefit. But then I let them add his name, and he would cash it and spend it on himself ... on booze. I would have to make sure that I cashed it first. It felt terrible. I went from being independent to having nothing at all. Also I had no one to talk to, no one to tell how I felt.

My family disowned me when I married Patrick. They refused to come to our wedding. I didn't want to tell them what was happening. I didn't want to give them the satisfaction of saying, 'We told you so.' I was one of six children. Most of them live locally.

I felt I had to be strong for my children's sake. I didn't have any friends at the time. I had lost touch with everyone. Our neighbours never spoke to us. I was very much on my own. My daughter was not attending the local school because it did not provide the subjects that she wanted, so that made it harder for me to meet people.

I lost custody of my second child to my first husband. He was successful largely because of all the problems at home with Patrick and his drinking and the violence. My son was 10. He did not want to go and live with his father. I saw him a couple of times not long after he left and then his father stopped me seeing him altogether. I didn't see him again until he was 15. He came to see me without his father knowing and I haven't seen him since. That was ten years ago. I wrote later and told him I was moving and gave him the address, but I don't know whether he got the letter or not. I am sure his father poisoned his mind against me. When I had custody the social services would take him down to see his dad and bring him back. But when his dad had custody and would not let me see him, social services would not help me. So I didn't have much faith in the system – although I had a good social worker when I needed a refuge to get away from Patrick.

I was on my own with the eldest and youngest children for about two months after I managed to get the injunction served on my husband. But he kept coming to the house. I had to call the police twice to arrest him for banging on my door and abusing me, and each time he was sent to prison. The second stretch was twice the length of the first. Then he discovered that if he wrote a nice letter to the court they would let him out. After about two months I had him back. He made all these promises and of course I wanted to believe him. People cannot understand that. They cannot understand how you feel. They say, 'Why do you bother?' But I loved him. I thought he was going to change. Everything was fine, but only for a couple of weeks. But I still had my own money. That was important to me because it meant I could keep my independence. I didn't have to ask him for every penny. I could buy what I wanted without him having to agree. It caused rows. Once I bought the kids a pair of shoes and he was furious. He told me how many bottles of cider he could've bought with it. His return lasted for about five months, until I went back to court to use the evidence I already had to get a divorce. Apparently the evidence is valid for up to six months and then you have to start all over again.

After I applied for a divorce Patrick moved to London and the children and I moved to another part of town. We got moved to a nice, big flat. I could do what I wanted. I had no one to answer to. It was lovely. I still didn't have much to do with anyone – not for a long time. I would talk to people if I saw them on the landing but I was never close to anybody. It was OK during the day but it was lonely at night, especially once my youngest had gone to bed. In fact I had been lonely for a long time – long before Patrick left. When we had all been together in our previous flat I hadn't spoken to any of the neighbours in the five years we had been there. Patrick had talked to some of the local men in the pub, but that was as far as it went.

After we separated life was very different. My family got back in touch with me. Although my brothers and sisters lived nearby they hadn't been in touch because my parents didn't approve of Patrick and they didn't want to go against them.

I no longer had any money problems. My rent was paid direct by Social Security. I had meters in the flat for my gas and electricity so I could put the money away each week. I could save money from my family allowance book and then go out and buy something. At this stage I only had one child at home. My oldest had left home and my second child was still living with his father.

After a couple of months my son fell and broke his leg. He wanted to see his father so I got in touch with Patrick again. He came and visited and then our son went and stayed with him for a couple of weeks. He had managed to get off the drink and stay off. In fact he has not had a drink for twelve years now. He is a completely different person. I think he used to say he was going to stop drinking as a way of shutting me up. But he managed to do it on his own. We gradually started talking to each other again. I would go to London and see him, but I was also free to return home when I wanted to. It was nice. I could go and visit him and if I got fed up I could just come back. I had nobody to tell me what to do any more and I was still in charge of my money.

Eventually we got back together again. He's quite different and so is our relationship. He works as a foreman on a building site and gives me an allowance for the housekeeping and one for myself. I can get what I want with that and he doesn't mind. I used to do child-minding, but I haven't done that lately. Also I haven't got the space here. At the moment I'm saving my own allowance for a trip to Australia. Before that I used to spend it on clothes or things for myself. I know I'm dependent on Patrick to give me money, but I feel it's OK. I don't mind because it comes every week regularly. If I had to keep asking him for money I think that would be different. He comes home from work and – depending on what mood he is in – he hands it to me or he just puts it on the table. Or sometimes he will get up first in the morning and say that he has left it on the kitchen table. It's given freely and I always get it.

We've been back together again for about twelve years. For the past ten years I thought we were divorced. I had no intention of getting married again. But I found out recently that we are still married. The solicitor apparently forgot to file for the divorce absolute so it didn't go through.

The whole basis of our relationship is different from the way it used to be. I kept my independence to start with by having my own place and my own money. When we started going out again together I wouldn't let him pay for everything. I didn't want him to think that I was relying on him for money. I paid my share. I thought if I let him start paying for things he would think that I needed him – that I was relying on him. I wouldn't go out with him – or anyone else – unless I could pay my share. He went from strength to strength. He bought a car. He had never had one before. He stopped smoking as well. He suffers with asthma. He had pains in his chest and I think that frightened him.

Life with Patrick is so much better now. Everything is different. He's much more generous than he used to be. We go out together, which we never did before. We couldn't afford to pay for both of us at the pub. We've got things now that we could never afford before. He is still careful with money, but that's OK. And everything is jointly owned. An insurance cheque arrived in the post yesterday with both our names on it. I'm now entitled to half of it and that makes me feel good. Before, it felt like he was the man earning all the money and I was not entitled to anything. I don't see why he should have everything and me nothing – not any more. I couldn't go back to living like that again.

Looking back I can't explain why or how I let all those things happen to me. I'm sure that being on my own was good for me. I won't let people walk all over me any more. If someone told me to do something I used to just do it. But now, if I don't want to do something, I won't. That goes for Patrick as well: years ago I would have automatically done whatever it was he wanted without even thinking about it. But that has all changed. I'm a much stronger person as a result and I like myself much more now. I feel much better about myself. I'm much more in touch with myself and my own needs and I'm no longer anxious to please other people. Being on my own helped me to believe in myself. It showed me that I could manage. Before that my husband had always led me to believe that I couldn't manage without him.

I haven't lost my independence since we have been back together. I know I still depend on him for money but that doesn't change how I feel about myself. I still do what I want and can disagree with him and that's all OK now. I can go out without him and that's OK too, whereas before it wasn't. If I asked him if I could go out, it would cause lots of rows – usually because he wanted to go out drinking. Now I just tell him I'm going out and it's fine. Our relationship is better now than it has ever been. He sees things differently. Everything no longer revolves around how much money he has got in his pocket to spend on drink – and how much I thought he might have. We used to lie to each other, especially over money. We trust each other now. I don't have to hide my money and if I need some I just ask him and he gives it to me.

Separation or divorce

What I needed most when I was being abused by my husband and living in debt was someone to listen to me. I didn't want to be told to leave him. I just wanted someone to listen. I needed to feel that I had some support, someone to talk to. I knew in my heart what I ought to do – and that was to leave him – but I didn't want anyone to tell me that. I needed to get there myself – to come to that realisation on my own. I also needed practical help and advice and that would've been the next step that would've helped me – as long as the person helping wasn't telling me that I ought to leave my husband. I already knew that.

One of the most important things for me was having some control over my own finances. That was a big step. And a great relief. It was the beginning of a different way of seeing myself. I felt much stronger. But you need to be ready for that. And that does not come about through people telling you to do this or that. It is something that just happens. For me it was unplanned. I remember it was all to do with a cheque for my daughter's grant that I had received from the education authority. She wanted the cheque to be made out to her but she would have gone out and spent it on something else. My husband said it should be his. He would have spent it on drink. I'd had enough. That was what triggered my leaving Patrick. I always thought it would be because he hit me and broke my bones, not something like this. I saw a solicitor, got the divorce under way and then managed to get a housing transfer out of the area.

Looking back, it changed all our lives for the better. I didn't realise it at the time, but I know that if I hadn't done this, my husband would not be alive today. He managed to change his whole way of life and especially to give up the drink and cigarettes. It was hard for me at the time feeling unsupported and not having any family around me, going to a strange place to live and not knowing anyone there. But it has been worth it. I have been through a lot with Patrick but we have moved on. You don't really forget and it's upsetting to remember it. We have never sat down and talked about what we went through. I think Patrick thinks I didn't suffer in any way because it was him who had the problems. I think he understands better now what I went through but it's not something we ever talk about. We've got a nice life now. I like my independence and my freedom. I've got choices over what I do and we have enough money to enjoy the little things in life. Although I am still dependent financially on my husband I can please myself about what I do. If I want to visit my sister in Ireland I will go and feel OK about it.

For further details see Chapter 12. Separation and divorce; and Chapter 14. Benefits for parents on low pay.

ALICE: PENSION RIGHTS IN DIVORCE SETTLEMENTS

Alice is a pensioner. She was divorced about a year ago after 40 years of marriage. I met her through an organisation called Fairshares, which was set up to campaign for a wife's automatic entitlement to a share of her husband's pension in a divorce settlement. Many of their members have suffered hardship after divorce because the pension was overlooked and many had been holding their breath – according to Dawn Barnett, who set up the organisation in late 1993 – in the hope that they could stave off divorce proceedings until a change in the law (which took place on 1 July 1996).

The Pensions Act will make it easier for divorcing couples to divide their pension assets between them, and a wife (or husband) will be able to 'earmark' her right to a share in her husband's pension when he retires. But groups like Fairshares believe the reforms should have gone further and will continue to campaign for 'pension splitting' – allowing the pension funds to be divided between the spouses on divorce – rather than 'earmarking', as this will mean the wife will be dependent on her ex-husband in retirement: her pension will start only when he retires and in many cases will cease when he dies. Pension splitting would also have the advantage of enabling former spouses to make their own, independent financial arrangements for their old age. Courts in Scotland have long been obliged to consider pension arrangements when drawing up final divorce settlements.

Alice, like a lot of women, was not given this option by her solicitor and the whole issue of her husband's pension was completely overlooked. As a result she – and other women like her – may have grounds for a negligence action against her solicitor. In the meantime her ex-husband is very comfortably off as a retired bank manager and Alice, like a lot of wives of her generation who devoted themselves to caring for their husbands and children, is living in debt on her pension – a few pounds short of eligibility for (and short of obtaining the added benefits of) Income Support.

Lord Simon Glaisdale summed up the situation in his comment to the House of Lords during the debate on splitting funds after divorce: 'In the ordinary way a wife makes sacrifices during the early years of the marriage, freeing her husband to pursue his economic advancement. It is utterly unjust to enable the husband to take that pension away from the wife who has enabled him to earn it and bestow it on some other woman who has found greater favour in his eyes.'

Alice's story fits a common pattern. 'Today's destitute divorcees', says Sally Quinn from Fairshares, 'were young married women in the days when unless you were super-rich you stayed at home and looked after your children. There were no crèches and nurseries. Wives were often abandoned at a time in life when it was too late to acquire the new skills which might have found them a job – and far too late to build a pension in their own right.'

I was divorced about a year ago after 40 years of marriage. My husband simply walked out one day. The reason I feel so aggrieved about the divorce settlement is because I made the mistake of not going to a proper divorce lawyer. I didn't realise at the time how important this was. Instead I saw a 'solicitor' whom I assumed was qualified but he turned out to be a legal assistant, although I was not aware of that at the time. He suggested divorce, which I did not want to agree to; I wanted a separation and had already suggested this to my husband as a way of saving money. I knew a divorce would be costly and take a long time whereas a separation would have meant that there would have been no costly letters going between us via our solicitors. The solicitor did not tell me that I could have insisted on a separation and now I have a very costly bill from him of at least £3,500, which I am unable to pay. My husband's bill is £2,800.

My husband suddenly left me about three years ago. At the time I felt there was a chance of some mediation rather than rushing into a divorce – perhaps also a more amicable ending to our relationship, maybe even some companionship in the long term. Also I needed to talk about it. I didn't want a divorce immediately. He just walked off after we had an argument over our daughter. He'd got really worked up after talking to her on the phone and then insisted that I deal with her. My daughter and I were both in tears after this argument and when I put down the phone I shouted at him to get out. It felt like the last straw. I couldn't take it any longer. It was me who brought the children up, not Richard.

He could never handle any difficulties with them and always left that and the disciplining to me. He always appeared the 'nice', loving parent in front of them. Neither of my children knew what he was really like. He often shouted at me to get out of the house. One night he pushed me outside in my nightie and locked me out for three hours. He's a violent man. It lies just below the surface. If you were to meet him you would say, 'What a nice man – a charming man.'

He was violent towards me even before we were married. On my wedding day my brother tried to persuade me not to marry him, but I couldn't let my mother down. Also the bridesmaid was downstairs. I remember my brother came upstairs to my room and I was sitting at my dressing table. He said, 'Please, please, take those clothes off. I'll take you to the station. I'll straighten things out here and then I'll come and take you away.' But I couldn't do it. Richard had hit me before we were married and also afterwards. I left him for three months after we had been married for five years. He used to drink a lot. I was working then and he used to come and pick me up and we would go straight to the pub. We'd be there from six o'clock until closing time every night and this went on for a few years. It meant I couldn't do anything – not even cook. If I hadn't gone with him there would've been hell to pay.

He had a responsible position in the bank. I've since heard that the female staff were frightened of him and wouldn't go down into the strongroom alone with him. I never really trusted him. He had a girlfriend soon after we were married. I remember we were invited to a dance and I sat at a table by myself all night because he danced with her all the time. On the way home in the car I said I'd wasted my time going to the dance, and with that he suddenly stopped the car, pushed me out then drove off at high speed. He left me to walk the fifteen miles home.

I never felt as if I had any power in our relationship. After six years of marriage and working, my husband decided that he didn't want me to go to work any more. He felt that my job was to be at home looking after the house. I had become very frightened of his temper and didn't want any more arguments, so I stopped working. It had been a marvellous job. I tended to fill in when other staff were away. I loved it. It was great. When I was working everything I earned went back into the house: the bills, the food. He didn't pay for a thing. But he didn't want me to have a life outside the house. He didn't want me to be independent. His pride was such that he didn't like his wife working. After that things didn't go too badly. He gave up drinking so much. It was 1964.

In all the 40 years that we were together I could never, ever discuss anything with him. Not even the subject of children. He never slept with me – only a few times in all those years. There were a lot of children available for adoption at that time so I decided to apply to adopt through a church organisation. I remember my husband would not answer me when I tried to tell him about the application, so I thought that if he didn't actually say 'No' and start shouting at me then that means it's OK. My husband was never interviewed by the adoption agency because he wasn't there during the day. The only time he was seen by them was at the final interview, but he didn't say a word. I did all the talking. All they asked him was, 'Are you keen on sport?' And he said he was. Within two weeks I had a telephone call to say they had a lovely baby boy five weeks old and would I like to come and see him? They didn't ask if *we* would like to come – only me. Anyway I said that I didn't want to see the baby first – I wanted him regardless! How can you go and 'see' a child? It was the same with my daughter, who came to us eighteen months later. I really enjoyed them and taught them both to read and write by the age of three.

My husband was never interested in the children. I'd encourage them to rush out when he came home and say to them, 'Go on, make a fuss of Daddy.' But once they started to do well at sport he became more interested in them. They were older then. My son did very well at cricket and my husband sometimes watched him play and would strut around the place. Our daughter did very well at sports too. But it was always me who did the running around.

I regretted not working and felt that I could've worked while the children were at school, but there were always rows every time I mentioned it so it wasn't worth pursuing it. During all this time I was being given only enough housekeeping for food, not clothes or anything else. I remember when my son went on a school trip to France and I sold some of my mother's jewellery to pay for it. He always refused to pay for things like that and said that he never went to France or whatever, so why should they? He forgets that he went to school during the war. It became a pattern that I'd try and pay rather than have a confrontation. I also felt strongly that as adopted children they should feel that they had two parents and would often tell them that their father was an honourable man

– even if he didn't play with them or take much notice of them. But of course it was all lies. I was lying! I knew he was seeing other women. But I felt that they should believe he was a good man. I think it's in a woman's make-up to want the best for her children.

The only way I could afford to buy the children's clothes – and my husband's – was through mail-order clubs and catalogues. I could stagger the payments and budget for them out of the housekeeping without him knowing. He never gave me money for clothing. I didn't like buying the children's clothes through catalogues. It would've been so much nicer to have gone out shopping with them. To buy them treats. Everything came out of the housekeeping, including Christmas presents, and yet I was paid very, very little. I inherited £5,000 from my mother when she died and that's how we managed to move house. It was 1968 and the children were 2 and 3. I couldn't stay in Kent after my mother died. We were very close and used to see each other every day. I put all my money towards buying a house. It was a lot in those days. But I didn't have any say in which house my husband bought. I did have some say in my car, though. It was a little Mini. It was a happy time to start with in our new house. He was still having affairs. I made the dreadful mistake of ringing him one night at his bank when he said he was working late. He hadn't been home before 9 p.m. or 10 p.m. for weeks and weeks. Even the children were complaining. He said he'd try to get home early this particular night but hadn't turned up. The bank manager said he wasn't working late and hadn't been working late at all. The next thing I knew he'd bought a brand-new car and said he needed to go away for the weekend to run it in. He admitted his lady friend was going away with him. When I said, 'What am I supposed to do?' he said, 'You've got your own car …'

He always bought things for himself without any discussion. I never had that option because, although we had a joint account, I never had a chequebook. When he retired he cashed in an insurance policy of £18,000. He also had another amount from his bank of around £20,000, which he frittered away, according to the bank statements that I saw later. I've since discovered that there was another endowment policy that he'd paid into but he didn't declare in his affidavit. There are also at least three other accounts that I've since found out about, but I was unaware of any of them at the time of the divorce.

I contacted an organisation called Fairshares, who put me in touch with a local solicitor and she has found out all this

Separation or divorce

information. Fairshares was set up to fight for women like me and to make sure that we get shared pension rights in divorce settlements. If that had been the case I wouldn't be in this situation and I would have had a much higher standard of living. As it is I am trying to live on £70 a week, which is very hard. It includes my pension of £58.92 and the rest is maintenance from my husband. That amount was decided by my husband's solicitor. I don't know how it was arrived at but he pays me £10 one week and £12 the next and so on. Sometimes he doesn't pay it, but instead will pay for the gardener which is £30 a month. The garden has to be kept up because the house is on the market and I couldn't possibly do it as I'm not able to physically. I don't remember being consulted about the amount of maintenance but I was very upset at the time of the divorce. I used to look out at the lovely view and it would make me feel very sad. Suicidal. I still feel like that at times. But how could I leave the dogs? They are my best friends.

I always tried to economise in our marriage. Now I'm in dire financial circumstances. I owe the solicitor at least £3,500 and that was mainly because of all the letters he wrote to my husband's solicitor, who didn't seem to answer them. I also have other debts which I have been trying to pay off, like the mail-order catalogue. That was outstanding before my husband went and he said he wouldn't have anything to do with it. I'm trying to pay them off at £45 per month. I can't remember the total but it's a lot. One reason I owe so much is that I've had to buy bigger clothes because I've put on a lot of weight recently because of my medication. Food here is very costly and although I'm lucky in that my local shop delivers goods, I know I'm having to pay far more for the food than if I bought it at a supermarket. A neighbour did some research for me and reckons I am paying £10 to £20 more a week, which is a lot out of £70. I've got these two big dogs as well who have been with me for years. Also I owe £70 on the telephone and I am £30 overdrawn at my bank.

I'm very isolated now because my husband took the car and I'm also asthmatic and arthritic. I tried to go into town on the local bus, but I can't manage it. The buses are a couple of hours apart and there's nowhere in town to sit down.

My new lady solicitor is very good and wants to help me as much as possible. She was thinking of taking my ex-husband to court for not paying the maintenance regularly – sometimes not at all. But I don't think I would stand much of a chance in court.

She has opened my eyes to a lot of things I didn't know. I thought there had been a clean break already. But it will not be a clean break until this house is sold. Also the maintenance agreement is flexible. I had no idea about that. It's index-linked, so that any increase in the cost of living is reflected in the payments he has to make. I have also discovered that I was wrongly advised on a number of other things, the most important one being that I could've refused a divorce. I wanted it to be more amicable over a two-year separation and I wanted us to meet on neutral ground.

I wouldn't be in all this debt now if we had done things differently and just taken our time over the divorce. Also I think that, personally, I wouldn't have felt so rejected. That's been devastating. It meant that I couldn't think straight. It feels like my contribution to the marriage and the family was nil. I said to my son recently, 'If it were not for the dogs I'd sooner be out of it.' It's not only the debts that distress me so much, it's my whole future: having to sell the house and probably move away. I've lived here for 21 years. I'll eventually get 70 per cent of the house, but it's been on the market for almost two years and no one has shown any interest in it. It's all so uncertain. I may return to Kent, where I grew up. My brother's wife is terminally ill and he wants me to go back there. But to leave here is going to break my heart. I won't be able to afford to buy anything after all the debts are paid. I shall have to rent. I don't think that reducing the price of this house – which my husband keeps insisting on and which has already been reduced by £15,000 – will make the slightest bit of difference because houses are just not selling here at the moment. The estate agent agrees with me.

I suppose all my debts must easily amount to £10,000. This also includes a grant that I got from the local council of £1,000 to do up the outside of the house because my income was so low, but as I'm moving I shall have to repay it if the house sells within a limited time. I don't know what's available in Kent but I'm sure that house prices are much dearer there than here. I expect I'll be able to pay all my debts when the house sells, but when will that be? It's hard to imagine how it'll feel to be free of the debts and the anxiety. It's awful knowing that I owe people money. I can't remember when I last had a proper night's sleep. I also get terrible stomach aches which I'm sure are stress-related. My health is definitely worse since my husband walked out. My doctor, who is also a friend, wishes there was more that he could do. He thinks my arthritis – which makes my knees swell up like footballs

Separation or divorce

– is all to do with the stress. All he can give me is painkillers, which I don't want to take. And I am already taking steroids through my inhalers for asthma. That's got a lot worse too.

I think it's very important to say to other women in a similar situation that they should go to court over the settlement – even if they are nervous. Apparently there is nothing to be nervous about. I made a big mistake by not going to court. When my husband thought I would be going, he started writing to me and ringing me for a while and then he said he didn't want me to go to court because it'd be too upsetting for me – and I believed him! I'm sure that I would've had a much fairer deal if I'd gone to court. I would've had a barrister who would've had my interests at heart. The other important point is not to allow yourself to get lonely – and to get support around you by using your friends to help. Unfortunately I didn't have any friends because my husband wouldn't mix with anyone and I never went out on my own. Obviously I would talk to people in the village, but not socialise with them. He wouldn't allow me to. If anyone came knocking at the door he would say, 'Oh, God! What do they bloody want?'

I am left feeling rejected and very, very lonely. He was a companion, even though we hardly spoke. I seem to have lost interest in a lot of things and the deterioration in my health doesn't help. And to go out into the village and socialise costs money. I just can't afford that. I feel awful that the villagers no longer come to me for cakes, but my food mixer has broken. I wrote and asked my husband for some money to have it fixed and his answer was, 'Hard luck. Tough.' I hate having to ask him for money and of course it goes very much against the grain to go cap in hand. I've always tried to economise – and I still do so now. He pays the electricity so I try to be careful not to use too much. During the winter I kept a duvet around me to save on electricity. When the bill arrived last time it wasn't properly sealed and I confess I took a peak. I felt awful doing it but I wanted to know how much it was. I discovered it was £170 in credit!

Having my new solicitor feels like a light at the end of the tunnel, if only I could afford the fee for legal aid. They want £24 before we even start and I can't afford that. Even if I qualified for legal aid I would have to pay £24 a month for as long as it lasts. So it may be that she is in a position to help me, but I am not in a position to pay her. However, they have assured me not to worry about it at the moment, but I can't help worrying about it. It would be lovely to be free of worry. But there is not much I can do until the house is sold.

I am anxious to see what happens when the new legislation governing pension assets of divorcing couples comes into effect. I might've benefited if the divorce had not been so rushed. I might've had a right to a share in my husband's pension when he retired as well as a widow's pension scheme offered by the bank where he worked. That doesn't mean I would necessarily have had a right to a share in his assets – only his occupational pension, which is quite considerable. But at least that would've been fairer. As it is it seems terribly unfair, but I think I knew that – and felt that – all my so-called married life. I did everything around the house – cooking, washing, ironing, decorating, gardening and economising – doing most of it quickly during the day so that when I picked up the children from school we could do things together. Looking back I realise that for 40 years I was really an unpaid housekeeper.

Unfortunately Alice has not benefited from the change in legislation regarding having a legal right to her ex-husband's pension, because the legislation came too late for her and it is not retrospective. She was seriously contemplating suing her former solicitor but the financial requirements of legal aid – the ongoing monthly fee, albeit small – that she would be required to make are prohibitive. Basically she cannot afford to sue him even with some financial assistance provided by legal aid.

For further details see Chapter 12. Separation and divorce; and Resources (Divorce).

3 Loans and grants

ISOBEL: SINGLE-PARENT STUDENT WHO SURVIVED

Isobel is a mature student. That means she is one of the UK's 750,000 students in higher education who had passed their 21st birthdays when they began their degree courses.

Isobel is also a single parent and has three children as well as a mortgage. Until 1 September 1995, students like her, who had children and mortgages and were aged over 25, were given a top-up grant of £1,070 a year. But that grant has now been withdrawn in spite of research which demonstrates that older students experience greater financial hardship than younger ones. They graduate with an average debt of £4,138 – 44 per cent more than the average younger student, who owes £2,884 according to a recent study by Barclays Bank. Another report (by the Committee of Vice Chancellors and Principals) quoted in the Observer *('Money Matters', 27 October 1996) shows that mature students are more likely to apply for hardship funds and to leave their courses prematurely.*

Government policy has ensured that student grants from public funds have diminished and instead a system of grants and loans has increased. Also most full-time students in higher education are now no longer eligible for state benefits.

All Isobel's children have studied or are studying at university, and as a result they have all been seriously in debt. This is the pattern of the future, when it is predicted that the cost of a university student's degree will soon be £20,000 (Guardian, 17 September 1996).

I am 55. I divorced eight years ago after 25 years of marriage, which was very traumatic. I managed to get a job but realised that I needed qualifications to get a decent wage so I decided to do an access course in order to get into university. The grant was minimal; it would've been impossible to live on, but I had just received some compensation for an accident I'd been involved in so the money I got kept me for that year. I also had a lot of debts. You can get further awards or grants at the college's discretion, but I didn't know that at the time.

I got an offer of a place from my local university and I was also eligible for a grant. That was very little as well and I wondered how I was going to cope on it. It was less than £4,000. I had managed to buy my own house after my husband and I had split up and the mortgage cost me about £200 a month. I also had two children still living at home. I was getting maintenance from my ex-husband but there was still a shortfall on the living expenses, running the house and travelling to university.

I wasn't eligible for a student loan because I was over 50. The government's justification for this is that if you're over 50 you're less likely to suffer hardship – but as an older student I have much greater responsibilities and don't have the same prospects in the workforce as a younger student. As a result, I've had to go into overdraft at my bank in the last few years and now have considerably more debts. I do see myself as economically productive. There are lots of things I'd like to do, like writing and counselling. I hope to be working for a long time. I'd like to be seen as useful and paying my way rather than people seeing me as a drain on society and leading the life of Reilly. Also I feel I've given a lot to others in my life in many different ways.

There are a lot of people who'd like the opportunity to study when they get older, or people like me whose circumstances change. I was married for 25 years and obviously maintenance wasn't going to cover everything – my maintenance was £10 a month. I'm angry about that because I helped him through his degrees when he was studying and supported him in his career. He had a very clever lawyer handling his divorce. He wouldn't agree to a divorce on the grounds of adultery unless I agreed to all sorts of conditions, including joint custody. I was far too soft. My solicitor wanted me to go for twice as much as I did, but I got terribly worn down by it all and my solicitor wasn't very good. I don't think he understood independent women. He saw them as an adjunct to males and their careers. He wasn't very sympathetic and I should've changed but he was supposed to be a friend. I had a very bad deal and so did the kids. Their father was very mean. He was living with a woman who kept saying things like I should go out and get a job. 'Why didn't I stack shelves at Tesco's?' I'd worked endlessly during our marriage. I had a curtain-making

Loans and grants

business, I worked in a school with handicapped children, always making clothes, I paid for all our holidays. He never paid for anything in the house – only the front room, which is the one that other people would see. He really only spent out on his car. I wasn't allowed to drive it for a long time. Looking back, I was a very, very useful wife. I made everything to save money. I made bread, cut everyone's hair, did all the decorating.

I got involved with local politics and got elected on to the local county council for eight years. On one of the committees I suggested that education grants should be assessed in a different way because I knew from the students and parents I talked to that there was a lot of hardship. I was on a huge number of committees in the end. I think that's why the marriage broke up. He was jealous of my success: all the phone calls, publicity. He accused me of neglecting the children, which wasn't true. He used all this against me in the divorce. He thought I ought to get a proper job, but I had no training or qualifications. I almost completed my training in working with handicapped children but I got pregnant and couldn't finish the course.

When I started my university course it became obvious that I was going to need lots of books, especially since the library had suffered cuts and books were therefore in short supply. Also I was studying for a joint degree. After my accident I developed a form of dyslexia, so I needed books as I took longer to write things, to get ideas. I was elected on to the Students' Union as mature Students' Officer and I had a lot of people who'd come to me with problems, mostly to do with money. Then I started having problems myself.

I applied to the university's Access Fund, which is a hardship fund for students. It was just before Christmas and I was really desperate because I thought my house was going to be repossessed. I hadn't kept up with the payments. My income wasn't enough. The grant is supposed to cover the repayments, but it didn't because I'd had to buy so many books. I wasn't aware that I could've asked the department for a bursary. They're very small for each department and those administering them are not necessarily skilled in detecting the genuine needy as opposed to those who have wasted their grants on beer. Also I was running a car and having to come in every day, which was very expensive. There was a travel grant available but applying for it was very, very complicated.

I tried to get a positive diagnosis confirming my dyslexia, as it would've meant a further grant of £1,500, but I would've had to pay £150 for the assessment. I even had supporting letters from my doctor and my lecturers, but they wouldn't waive the fee. You get it back if you're successful, but I couldn't afford to take that risk. Also I was being investigated or medically assessed as I was involved in a second accident which I had two years to the day after the first accident in 1987. I was expecting big damages because of the disabling effects and ongoing pain.

My maintenance and grant totalled about £6,000 a year, but to run the house and car, repay the mortgage and maintain the children took about £8,000. If I'd had a student loan I would've had legitimate recourse to the Access Fund. As it happens, I applied for it anyway and managed to get two grants in two years. The money went immediately on repaying debts. I've found out there are quite a few grants and charities I could've applied to, but I was also trying to study for my degree. These things take time and energy.

Money has been a constant worry, trying to make do or to cut back on things. My telephone, for instance, wasn't a luxury, it was a lifeline. In the last five years I've been so depressed and desperate about things, including money, that I've rung the Samaritans and may not have done that if I'd had to ring from a phone box. It also meant I could phone my friends, otherwise I might've gone off my head.

Not having enough money has had a strange effect on me. I get into a kind of apathetic mood. I become very fatalistic – nothing matters anyway. I can't solve the problem or pay the debt and then I get desperate. I got into a real state about filling in forms. I couldn't cope. It was so hard trying to manage everything and I was doing too much at once. My joint degree was the whole of philosophy, as if I was doing a single honours degree, and two courses of theology. I had to give up philosophy. I failed the exams and in the end I had to take a year off. I was also travelling in each day so there was no respite. I was overloaded academically and emotionally and had all these financial worries, including twice being threatened with repossession.

I did spend a lot on books – hundreds of pounds. That might seem irresponsible, but I couldn't see any other way. I had a lot of trouble taking down the notes in lectures because of the dyslexia, and I had to buy a dictating machine, which made things easier. But there was always the trauma of another bill

Loans and grants

appearing just after I had settled one bill, having managed to get the money somehow, and it was like going into shock for a few days after receiving it. I always seemed to be borrowing money and then trying to pay it back. It was an ongoing nightmare.

There is a financial adviser at university and I found her incredibly helpful. I went to see her a couple of times, usually when I'd left things for too long, hoping that they would go away, like not answering letters. That's been a big thing for me – not opening my mail and dealing with things at the time because I knew I couldn't pay the bills. But at the same time I knew that if I didn't deal with things it would be far worse. I got into a state where I couldn't open my phone bills because I knew they were going to be large. I'd spend time on the phone talking to people about the stress of it all, but it actually wasn't getting things done. It's quite common for people like the adviser to have someone like me coming to her at the eleventh hour and saying, 'Everything's going to be cut off and I'm about to have my house repossessed,' when they should've gone to her ages before that happened. You tend to avoid it as though it's going to go away. I can help other people to fill in forms, but when it comes to doing my own, I just push them away. It's something I feel very stupid about.

I contacted the Samaritans several times because I couldn't go on any longer with the pain of it all. There's not a lot of sympathy for students – people think you live a life of luxury. My next-door neighbour says I should get a proper job and then I'll find out the realities of life. Meanwhile she is cocooned in her sheltered existence, with a husband who helps her to hang out the washing!

A lot of my friends at university are in a different situation. Their debts don't seem as serious as mine, which are about fear of repossession and also not having the same prospects as them in the workforce. They're much younger than me and don't have the same kind of responsibilities, especially financial ones. I don't resent that at all. Often they have only to pay rent. Also a lot of them have parents whom they can just ring and ask for financial help. I was forced to borrow £50 last year for my electricity. I was desperate, so I asked my brother who is extremely well-off. He did lend it to me, but seemed quite reluctant. I felt terrible about having to ask him for it; we don't get on all that well and it was humiliating. The electricity board was threatening to make me use a key meter. You have to take this card to the local depot and pay so much and then get it charged up. You really are poor when you do that and you'll never get a meter back again. The idea is that you pay more for your electricity because they are deducting arrears at the same time. I need to use a lot of electricity because part of my disability means that I can't hang up washing. I need to use a tumble dryer and that costs a lot.

I have a wealthy 'friend' who paid a bill for me but obviously I couldn't keep doing that. In fact she bought a half-share in my house as a way of trying to 'help' me. Although she has been very, very kind in bailing me out several times, I feel my independence is yet again diminished. The house is still in the same poor shape and I'm a lot worse off because she now owns half my house and I've got nothing much out of it. She's still got power and control over me and comes round and tells me things, like I should have a lodger.

I very much wanted someone to take care of things at that time, to take responsibility for all the debts, especially the house. Also I was very vulnerable. Things were so desperate that I actually didn't want to live at the time.

After the end of my first year at university I was thoroughly exhausted, mainly because of all the financial problems. That was the year I had off. I can't remember much of that year, except I wasn't paying many bills and keeping the bank at bay with assurances that I'd be getting a sizeable amount in damages as a result of my (second) accident. I don't think I did anything useful in that year. I escaped into television a lot and I had to write six essays for university. I was on Disability Allowance all that year because of depression and then I went on to Invalidity Allowance. I was prescribed anti-depressants. The money situation was worse because the Disability Allowance was less than my grant. I had to pay Council Tax as well. I seemed to spend a lot of time going to Social Security and chasing around after money.

Looking back at this year off, I should've got a job. I think I was falling back on my helplessness. I was locked into it and getting free prescriptions and anti-depressants and painkillers.

I had exceeded my overdraft limit of £3,500, so by the time I got my damages claim £3,500 had to come off it. I had a legal aid bill of around £3,000. On top of that I lost another £5,000 because I had to repay my Disability Allowance from the previous year because of my damages award, even though the reason I was on disability had nothing to do with the accident. I wasn't aware I would have to repay the allowance. My solicitor should've known this and has apologised. If he had known, then he could've asked for proportionately more damages. He told me I could always go to another solicitor and sue him. I'd seen about eight consultants for both sides over a five-year period. I was told I would get between £30,000 and £50,000, which would've been fair. Any kind of effort, physical and mental, takes a toll on me and I'm often in pain. I was awarded £16,500 and after paying out various people I had very little left.

The anxiety of having debts as a student has affected my study quite profoundly. I feel as though I've only half-achieved my potential on the course. It's affected my ability to absorb and to concentrate on my studies and that makes me angry. I know I'm capable of getting a first-class degree. And I'm sure there are lots of others like me who, had they not had money problems and family commitments, would've done a lot better.

Being a student and a single parent has its own set of problems, and although my children wanted to go to university, they did so reluctantly because they'd seen what I went through and had been part of that financial hardship. They didn't want to be a burden to me. Also student children of single parents don't enjoy the same advantages as those with two parents – particularly where those parents are supporting them financially.

The same kinds of issues that I experienced have arisen for my children when they were students at university. They've had to interrupt their studies and work at nights, weekends and holidays. In fact my son seriously considered not becoming a student because of his mother's and sisters' financial experiences. My ex-husband would perhaps pay the occasional fiver towards their upkeep.

When I look back at his financial contribution it is appalling. He didn't pay anything after he left, including the mortgage repayments. He went off with another woman in 1986. He would come over every now and again and give me £25 for the children. I was dependent on my expenses allowance from the council. That was all I had. In the meantime he bought himself a smart car and we were threatened with repossession. The children were aged 20, 17 and 10 and they were all dependent. My oldest daughter had just started at university. They were traumatised by his leaving. The house was on the market for a long time and I persuaded the bank that it would eventually sell. When it was sold there were £11,000 of debts and arrears. They were mostly his. He was very well-off at that stage and so was his partner. They were both in full-time, well-paid jobs. Fortunately I had enough to put down as a deposit on my own house – even though it is now co-owned.

My first daughter is now aged 30 and she's still paying off her student overdraft. My second daughter is about to finish her degree at university. She's more conservative with her money, but I have just found a letter saying she owes £394 for gas, and she owes rent as well. She was working as well as studying. She was earning £10 a night working in a theatre. She was told she'd get tips but she didn't. She was so affected by her debts that she took a year out as well. She said she didn't want to do her third year with all the debts she had. The student grant in no way matches the expenses they have. She's studying sculpture and ceramics and they have to pay for all their materials as well as studio fees. She has lots of debt, although she's always had a job. She'd like to further her studies – and is being encouraged to do so by her tutor – but there is no way she can afford to. As a single parent I'm unable to help much financially. In the meantime she's working in an unsuitable job and her artistic talents are going unused.

My son is in his first year at university and has worked in a supermarket for the past three years. He's seen how financial difficulties have affected us all and is keen to be self-supporting. Unfortunately his father has reduced his maintenance. My son is keen to pay off his overdraft by working full-time in the holidays. I don't know how much it is. He hasn't told me. He also has a student loan, which is approximately £3,500.

We all seem to have been plagued by money problems as students. And it feels like there's no end in sight. My older daughter had to borrow as a student in order to live and left university with an overdraft of £5,000. The bank has got her trapped. I lent her some money towards a deposit on a rented house she was sharing with a friend and bought her a lot of clothes when she got her first job, as she had nothing suitable. She's had three jobs since she left university. Her first job was selling insurance. That was all there was available to graduates at the time. What is this government doing to our educated young people? It's so destructive in terms of their potential. My daughter is working largely on commission. A lot of employers now are taking on staff on temporary contracts. Everything has changed. My daughter is part of an aggressive world of business and I think money has dominated her life – right from my money problems, then all of us being students and having to pay bills and her not having the sort of parents who could (or would) help her financially. She still has her overdraft and tells me she would like to have children but she cannot afford to.

Loans and grants

Since our interview Isobel has graduated from university with a BA honours degree. She was disappointed that she did not get a first-class degree and felt she could have achieved better if she had not been plagued by money worries.

She left university owing approximately £3,500, which she was able to pay off with the money from her damages claim. She was also given an overdraft limit of £1,000 in her student account.

She worked part-time doing night work in an old people's home, had a period of signing on, sent off over 200 job applications, was short-listed thirteen times, completed a computer course paid for by a friend and has managed to secure a job – part-time and temporary – 60 miles away from home, costing £56 a week in travel. The job is likely to become permanent and enable her to pursue further studies. She is delighted.

For further details see Chapter 18. Being a student.

LISA: SINGLE-PARENT STUDENT WHO DID NOT SURVIVE

Lisa's story highlights the difficulties for a single parent determined to pursue further education and at the same time trying to combine study with child care in an unsupported and impoverished environment.

Lisa was expected to live on her grant, which meant that she was not entitled to any state benefits. She became so desperate that at one point she asked social services to take her children into care as she felt she could no longer manage to feed and care for them adequately. She had virtually no help from anyone, not even from her children's grandparents. The relationship with them and her extended family ceased to exist after the breakdown of her marriage. It was as if the children were no longer important or no longer existed, leaving the family isolated and vulnerable.

Lisa struggled to put herself through college, but could not afford to complete the course. This compounded her sense of failure and her suicidal feelings. But eventually, with the help of an adequate income, she has been able to pay off all her debts. Looking back, she wishes she had left college much sooner and avoided the relentless cycle of debts, borrowing money, further debt and despair. That has all changed. Now she has savings, a good job and is thinking seriously about buying a house.

I got into debt gradually. I'd stopped working after having my second child. My husband and I had both been working up until that time. We'd always had rows about money, partly because I had to work as well as look after the children. It was always a hassle. He worked nights and wouldn't give it up to help look after the children because of the extra money he earned working those hours. It felt like he wasn't interested enough in his kids. Also he'd waste the money he was earning – usually on himself. I remember he bought some boots for £160 and a black suede jacket for £200. He also bought really expensive toys for the children that cost £70 and more and they were far too young to appreciate them. Also they didn't need them. And he bought useless things out of catalogues. So while he was strutting around in expensive clothes and the kids were playing with all these wonderful toys I didn't know where the next packet of nappies was coming from.

My husband expected that I'd pay for everything – including buying him a car – because I was working. He kept what he earned for himself. I think I thought that as he was the major breadwinner his money should be spent differently – on more important things – and as I earned less I should pay for extras like his driving lessons. My only luxury was plants. My front room looked like a greenhouse, but I loved them. Occasionally I would buy plants and planters. I also loved lizards which I'd bought. One day he came home and got angry about something – I think he accused me of overspending on food and smashed up all the plants and pots. At that time I'd managed to bring the food bill down to £15 a week. This was 1989 – the year we split up.

I decided to go to college a few months before we split up and got a personal grant which was given to people who are studying and living with a partner but get their own allowance for expenses for books and travel to college. That worked out to be £40 a week. It was in our joint account and my husband cashed it. That meant I couldn't buy any books, couldn't travel to college, couldn't pay anyone to look after the children. It was also the end of our relationship. He had become abusive and had violent outbursts, particularly when he was drunk. We split up not long after that, in December 1989. We'd been together for six years.

I was in dire straits financially. My ex-husband didn't give me any money and I had no cash for three months, as my next grant wasn't due until February the following year. I wasn't eligible for any financial help from anywhere because I was on a single person's grant of £40 a week. I tried to get help from the Social Security but they said my husband was still in a position to help with money. When they approached him he told them

Loans and grants

that he was giving me £100 a week and they believed him. They didn't even ask for any proof. They just refused to help me. In fact he has never paid anything at all towards the children's maintenance.

I was desperate. It was nearly Christmas. My only source of income was Child Benefit and I borrowed money against that from friends and then against my grant which was not due until February. I had no one to turn to and I felt very alone. The three of us were living on about £10 a week. My children were then aged 6 and 4. The phone had been cut off and they were threatening to cut off the electricity. I owed the council arrears on my rent. I had an agreement to pay off so much a week, but I hadn't kept to it. It felt as though no one cared. Even when a friend invited us for Christmas I declined as I thought she was only asking because she felt sorry for us.

We got through Christmas making decorations and cards for friends. We had no money for presents so we wrote poems for each other with pictures. I was really upset that I couldn't buy the children any presents, but they were happy and that made me cry. We didn't see anyone from their father's family. Apparently they'd been told all sorts of weird stories about things I'd done to my ex-husband!

I worked most evenings and paid for child care. There were always bills to pay. The money was peanuts and it didn't really help much. I was permanently exhausted. This went on for about eighteen months and by that time I was up to my neck in debt – I had rent arrears and was not getting help from anywhere. I wasn't eligible for help from Social Security because my grant was supposed to cover my living expenses and it was paid to me in advance – I had already received it from the beginning of the year. I wasn't getting any maintenance at all from my ex-husband and I was desperate.

I applied to various charities that help women to study and managed to get several small amounts of around £25 which was a help. My grant didn't arrive until the end of March. By this time I owed friends quite a lot of money as I had to borrow even more money against it because it was late in coming. I also owed money in rent. So when it finally arrived I'd had to use it to repay everyone as well as using it for all of us to live on.

I tried to economise as best I could. We were living on about £10 a week for food. We lived without any heating, as I knew that the central heating bill would be expensive and I was worried that my electricity was going to be cut off. The rent arrears were a real worry and I was eventually threatened with eviction because I still hadn't paid off anything towards the rent arrears.

I had no real support from anyone. Both my parents were dead and my brother was unemployed. Also he was angry that I'd left my husband and he wouldn't have anything much to do with me after we split up. It was the same with my ex-husband's family. They wouldn't have anything to do with me either. The only friends I had at that time lived along the balcony in the same block of flats. They would lend me money but expected to be paid back the following week, which I was not able to do.

I didn't grow up around here. It was the loneliest time of my life and it got worse instead of better. I didn't have any close family or friends to help me or to tell me that everything was going to be all right. The only people who gave me any encouragement during the time I was at college and in so much debt were a couple of community workers who worked on the estate where I lived. In fact they were the ones who suggested that I should go to college. They encouraged me because they'd seen me get things done on the estate. It was a nightmare there – kids falling out of windows, burglaries, muggings, there was even a siege. We wanted a caretaker, locks on the windows and a proper security system. The tenants had been trying to get this for fifteen years and somehow I managed to get it done. These community workers encouraged me to do the same course as they'd done, which gave me a tremendous boost. It was the first time in my life that I felt strong and capable.

Throughout the course they lent me sums of £200 and £300 to try to help me get through the time until I received my grant. But although they helped me financially and I was grateful I also felt quite threatened by them because I knew that they wanted their money back and I couldn't leave the course because I'd be letting them down. Also if I wasn't able to repay them we wouldn't be friends any more.

The course also brought up lots of other feelings for me, especially about my self-confidence. I'd always done very menial jobs, like working in factories. I met my husband when I was 16 and had my first child at 17. He regarded me as having a pretty face but no brains, and I believed him. I did OK at school but we were always on the move because my parents had died and the families we went to live with couldn't handle us, so we were always moving on. My mum died when I was 10. I went to sixteen infant and junior schools and five senior schools as well as a

Loans and grants

truancy school. I was on probation at 13. My husband was the first person who ever took an interest in me, so I believed everything he said.

I guess I mostly felt that the whole world was against me – especially when I was on my own with the kids. I often felt suicidal. At every turn there was something else. No matter how many letters I wrote to people explaining my situation I got no help. I was absent from college quite a bit because I became ill. My tutor used to let me use the phone at college to make it easier for me to contact people that I owed money to. I think he was quite worried about me.

This went on for two years. My grant was £80 a week and when it arrived I used it to pay everyone back. I managed to pay a little off the bills each week but my money had disappeared long before the end of each term. Then I'd have to go back to borrowing and scrounging again. I felt like a leech. I started to hide away from people. I hardly went to college, partly because I couldn't afford the bus fares to get there and also because I was always borrowing other students' books. I was always asking people for things.

I became extremely depressed, although I didn't let it show. Instead I joked about things. In reality I hated everything but I couldn't blame anyone or anything so in the end I turned it on myself. I stayed in the house as much as I could and hid from people who knocked on the door. If I saw anyone in the street I knew, I'd ignore them so they wouldn't ask me how I was. A few friends would ask me out but I thought it was because they felt sorry for me, so I wouldn't turn up. I thought seriously about suicide as the best way out and yet I couldn't bear the thought of how it would affect the children. I knew what it was like having no parents and what it would be like for them if I was not there. I thought that perhaps the best way out would be for them to go into a home somewhere and for me to be out of it altogether.

I went to social services for child care originally, but got no help. By the following summer I had asked them to take the children into care. By the time my March grant came through and I had paid off my bills I was left in the same situation again. I didn't think the grant covered me for the summer holidays so I went to Social Security to sign on and they refused because they said it was an annual grant which should include the holidays. In the end they gave me a grant of £4.95 per week![*]

[*] Lisa later appealed successfully against this amount and received a cheque for £240.

I was in tears in the office. It was so humiliating. I remember I cried all the way home. I called in at a friend's house and told her and then her husband came in and said he'd just spent £6 on a hairbrush!

By the end of the holidays the kids were both in nursery and had free school meals, which was a relief. They were being fed properly. My ex-husband was turning up drunk and hassling me and the children, so I decided to move house. The new place was lovely and it was very close to college. I didn't have the cost of travelling or paying for child care because I was able to be home when they finished school. Life in many ways became a lot easier. But financially it got harder and the pressure of college became worse. I couldn't stand the strain of all the assignments. The major problem was my neighbour's noise. She would play her music really loudly every night, all night until about five o'clock in the morning. She was eventually fined £1,000 for noise pollution. But in the meantime I couldn't sleep. I couldn't concentrate at college or do my assignments at home because of the noise she made.

In the end I had to leave college. My sanity was at stake. It affected the children as well. The police were often called but they couldn't get any answer when they knocked at her door. It was hopeless. It felt like no one could do anything about it.

Financially I was still in a mess. My suicidal feelings seemed more difficult to fight this time. What I needed was a close friend. Just one person that I could talk to, someone to reassure me and to tell me that suicide would not help anyone – that there was a light at the end of the tunnel; someone I could share my problems with. On the other hand I felt so bad I didn't want to burden anyone.

I see being in debt as owing say £300 or more. By the time I had finished college I owed about £3,000. That included my rent arrears and I was threatened with eviction again as well as having my electricity and gas cut off. It was terrifying.

My brother and I became close again when I left college. He hadn't made contact with me for quite a while after I split up with my husband. He realised what effect being on my own with all these debts was having on me and organised for someone to call round every day to see me. He would get them to bring something, like a pint of milk and some sugar. They'd stay all day until the kids came home from school. I didn't know what was going on to start with – all these people calling round. I realised later that my brother was afraid I was going to commit suicide. I had left college because I couldn't afford to stay on. They wanted me to take another year to repeat some of the work, but I had exhausted all my grant money and didn't feel I had any choice. I had to leave.

I was really angry to start with. It seemed like I'd been through all that hardship – and put the kids through it as well – and it was all for nothing. I had no qualification at the end of it. College had been central to my life and now I had nothing. Everything was focused on my getting the qualification – all the child-care arrangements, everything. Our whole lives were structured around it. When I finished college I still had no money and no job. I remember I spent three or four weeks at home doing absolutely nothing all day. Sometimes I would spend all day in bed.

I don't know how much the children were affected by my being in debt. They were very young when the debts started piling up. They were always very understanding. At Christmas when there was no one else there they were lovely. We had no television or anything and it was just the three of us, but they were great. They never complained. I still find it hard not to give them the things that they want – or that I think they should have. I am still trying to make up for all the things that they had to go without. They insist they don't want things but I suspect they are too scared to ask me because they think that I can't afford it.

Everything is very different now. After I left college I eventually signed on and managed to save my Child Benefit. As a result I was able to buy all the things we needed: a washing machine, a tumble dryer, a cooker, a fridge. I got the stuff at the furniture projects that they run for claimants. It's all second-hand but good.

I'm now in a regular job and I have a salary of £10,000 a year plus Family Credit plus Child Benefit, which works out about £40 more a week. The children are older and can take care of themselves after school. They are 11 and 13. I have just recarpeted the house, totally redecorated it and hired a gardener! I have also bought a car and today I've had an electric shower fitted. Now I'm looking for a house to buy. It has taken a long time to get to this point. I still get depressed sometimes and feel a little bit suicidal – that 'world hates me' feeling is still there. Also I am often reminded that I owed people money, and that makes me feel embarrassed – that somehow I had failed. I still get letters and they also make me feel that I've failed – that I'm incapable of looking after my own children – that I had put myself in this position; it was my debt. I had to pay.

I've got a good relationship with my boyfriend and I think that's got a lot to do with his being there for me. He's a nice guy. It's a very different relationship from the one I had with my husband. He's very supportive and keen for me to do the things that I want to do – like writing. He's helped me to heal.

Last summer we spent almost every night sleeping in the garden. We didn't have a tent. Just the quilts outside on the grass sleeping under the stars. He surrounded the garden with candles. He makes me feel like I can do anything – whatever I want. He can help to make things happen.

Now, looking back, I know what I need to do to deal with all the feelings of being in debt and depressed. I haven't done it yet. I feel strong. Before I was strong only in a physical sense, but now I am strong emotionally as well. I no longer close off all my feelings. I now know what love is! I think my strength has come from facing my problems. I used to feel hurt, embarrassed and totally incapable. At the time it felt as if everyone was against me and what was I doing? I was struggling all the time. I coped inasmuch as I didn't take it out on the kids. I took it out on myself. I didn't care – even when I was crossing the road – about what might happen to me. I'd often just walk straight out into the road without looking. I didn't take care of my appearance. I didn't brush my hair or care what I looked like. I was very skinny as I had lost loads of weight. But I didn't care about anything. I also had a period of not going to sleep. I refused to go to sleep because I knew that if I did I'd think about all the things that I had to do – the washing, the kids to sort out in the morning. So I didn't go to bed. The longest I stayed up without going to bed was two weeks. The woman next door was playing her music all night then. I was still at college.

I spent a lot of energy making sure that no one knew what I was thinking or feeling. I didn't trust anyone. I didn't tell anyone anything or share my feelings with anyone. This went on for about two or three years. You don't want people to know how bad it really is. You start to imagine that they're thinking all kinds of things – that they might take the kids. You get paranoid. Losing the kids was a big fear, although in the end I wanted them to be looked after. It was a last resort. Being a student didn't help either. Everyone in the flats thought students were lazy bastards. A waste of time. I didn't really identify with being a student. I felt different from everyone else. I felt that I belonged to a sub-class of people like alcoholics or the homeless.

I think things happened to me because I wasn't devious enough and not because I was emotionally vulnerable. There were ways that I could've got myself out of the financial mess that I was in – fraudulent things like working while I was on the dole. Knowing the system. But I was desperate.

If I was asked to suggest how best I might advise a woman in a similar position the first thing I would do would be to introduce her to the local female youth and community workers who work in most towns and cities around the country. DSS and social services tend not to give you the information that you need, but they will be able to help. You should be able to get names and addresses of organisations, where to go for free legal advice, benefits, grants, possibly even holidays for single parents. Our local workers have a house-swap system for women, which means they can escape, get away without having to go to a refuge.

There are so many issues involved in being a woman in debt. I came up against a lot of prejudice just being a single parent. People thought that because I was on my own that I was a scrubber. I had made my bed so I should lie on it. It just makes things seem so much worse at the time. More effort should be put into training people who have contact with the public to understand and manage them better, particularly when they are vulnerable like I was. Also there should be no discrimination where services are concerned. I know of someone who was offered all kinds of services simply because he was a father on his own with four kids. They offered him free child care and further education so he could learn a job that he could do from home. I don't know of any female single parents who have had that offer.

I certainly played a part in my situation. I should've given up college much sooner and gone out and got work. Any work. But I felt that I couldn't leave because I owed people on the course money and I didn't want to let them down or to feel a failure. I felt under a lot of pressure to stay. My kids liked me being a student. They were proud that I was more than a housewife. But I wish I'd known the system better, how it works, what benefits I was entitled to and what resources were available to women like me.

The other thing I wish I'd done was to take my ex-husband to court – to sue him for every penny he had! I've never received any money from him apart from one tenner, and in many ways I regret not having gone to court for maintenance. It was sheer arrogance and pride on my part that we've had no financial help from him so it's my own fault that we've got nothing. Actually I didn't realise that he had any money, but I was wrong.

I still resent the fact that he took my car that I'd paid for. I should've got it back and sold it and made money for me and the kids that way but at the time I didn't want anything to do with him. He'd come round drunk and hassling me, so it was easier to be free of him. Also I didn't want him having any rights to the kids. If he paid maintenance he would've felt he had a right to see them and it would've been harder to stop him seeing them if he'd been contributing to their upkeep.

At the time I was very young and naïve. I could've benefited from all kinds of help, especially advice on how to manage everyday things like bringing up the kids. I also could've benefited from some kind of instruction on how to budget, how to manage money. Also I lacked knowledge of how people lived. I had no blueprint. No model.

For further details see Chapter 12. Separation and divorce; and Chapter 18. Being a student.

4 Business failure

REBECCA: BANKRUPTCY, REPOSSESSION AND MORE DEBTS

Rebecca started a clothing design business in the mid-1980s when it was easy to borrow money. She saw a gap in the market and gradually began to build up her business. She enjoyed the creative side, but found the business side more of a challenge. She learnt as she went along and realised too late that running a business requires a great deal of skill and knowledge – a vital need really to understand business before embarking on it, to know how to anticipate difficulties and to solve problems. She also encountered a lot of prejudice as a woman in business and while she would not attribute her lack of success to this, she felt that the whole ethos of women not expecting to understand business was a powerful burden to carry.

Rebecca's business – like a lot of small businesses – ultimately failed. She and her husband were forced to declare themselves bankrupt and to sell their home. There are still debts outstanding four years later. She still feels enormous guilt and responsibility and profound regret. The stress and strain on her and her family has been devastating. She likened the loss of the business and its effect to a bereavement.

Recent figures suggest that of approximately 446,000 businesses which start up each year just 25,000 are still operating three years later. Almost half of these (45 per cent according to 1994 figures) were initiated by people under 34.

I started a clothing design business in 1985. I was like a lot of women at that time who were creative with good ideas and thought I knew best. Starting a business was not particularly difficult and banks encouraged you to borrow. Nevertheless it was frustrating as a woman dealing with the banks. I used to call it 'the Boutique Syndrome': 'Does your husband know what you are doing?' With hubby's approval the wife could have her own 'little' business and the bank seemed very happy with that.

In the clothing business it's almost impossible to make money on a small scale and this is where I think so many women will continue to make mistakes. If they are clever they can make money doing one-off designer knitwear or dresses or whatever. But labour (even your own) and materials cost a great deal and the chances are that, realistically speaking, the selling price of the garment produced will not allow a sensible profit margin. It's a classic catch-22 situation: people start because they see a need or a gap in the market – usually through their own experiences, like a need for their children to have cotton pyjamas because of eczema and so on. To start with, sales might be acquired through other like-minded mums, and you think you have a business. Chances are that during that time you will be forgoing any money yourself, so already the costing is out of true.

Like a lot of other women I saw a need and began to design and manufacture children's clothes on a small scale. I thought it was going to be a doddle because so many people really liked the clothes, the word was spreading and the response was very encouraging. I employed first one person, then a second, and gradually built a party-plan-based system of selling. What I failed to comprehend was the vital need to really *understand* business. I learnt everything as I went along. I drifted. I now get quite zealous about getting people to try to grasp what it is they are getting into before they are in so deep that they have not even time to think about it. And that can be difficult because they are bubbling with ideas and they think that all they have to do is to fill that gap in the market and go on producing these clothes. Of course this is all in hindsight!

I do feel strongly that people going into business should have a basic training in business skills, especially in a creative industry. Chances are they won't be able to read a spread sheet. All they want to do is to get through the interview with the bank manager and come out the other side alive. I think people should be taught in schools and colleges to budget and to understand basic business concepts of costing and so on to prepare them should they choose to go into business. Even if a student is going to be an employee, knowing about how to cost a garment, their time and so on, benefits everybody, including the employer, and particularly those individuals who choose to go into business for themselves.

Most important of all, I think that some form of recognised basic business knowledge should be a condition of a bank/building society business loan. I know it would be unpopular, but in the long run it would save a lot of heartache. You might think you do not need it, but you do. It's like driving. You can't allow people to drive on the open road without having passed a driving test. In the same way I think you should have to master the skills involved in running a business. After all, you are putting people in charge of other people, money, huge responsibilities. You get into a car and think you can drive it but you need to learn the skills to do it; it's the same in business.

One of the depressing things about all this is that people genuinely do have exciting and intelligent ideas and so often these go to waste with all that energy and potential, simply because of a lack of business acumen.

There are various enterprise agencies that have been set up around the country specifically to generate job creation. In theory they provide appropriate help and advice. Although there are many dedicated and extremely able people staffing these agencies, there are also many characters who have found their way into these jobs – who have the time to do this kind of work – because they themselves are either retired or have left their own particular line of work. In my experience those who had retired were often quite simply out of touch and their advice was retrospective and irrelevant. In many ways I am a classic example of the sort of person employed by these agencies: available because my business failed! After all, if you were successful in business you would be too busy to work there. I'm sure that they want people to succeed in business but some of them carry with them a burden of failure and as a client there is a risk of being affected by this attitude. You need people to be motivated for success. Of course you need caution, too, just like you need a handbrake when you're driving a car – and sometimes you need to use it – but not this culture of despair that we seem to have created.

A good example of this was when I went to my local development agency to get financial support to train someone who I thought had great potential. You would've thought they would be falling over backwards to help, since training is what the government promotes, but what they said was, 'We don't have budgeting for that particular thing right now but we could give you money for marketing. You put your money into producing a brochure and we'll sell you the services of a (private) consultant.

We'll meet the cost halfway.' Suddenly you find yourself paying £2,000 for someone to advise you to do something that you didn't want to do in the first place. This consultant's only link with the rag trade was that his wife worked in a dress shop and he had been a sales rep. for the car industry!

The most frustrating thing about these development agencies is that they act as agents for various different funds. If you fail to have a good relationship with your local agency then you simply can't go elsewhere. It's pot luck as to the service you get in your own particular area.

As a woman trying to get all these grants I found I was continually up against prejudices and assumptions. One interview I had culminated with the chap from the agency asking me what I had been doing in 1984, as it had already been established that I was the mother of a toddler and a baby at that time. I was then advised to 'get on with what you know best, dear'. As he left I childishly kicked the door for quite a long time! In fact he had a point. I didn't have a clue about business at that time. What a difference it would have made if he had simply arranged for me to get constructive advice as to how to *do* the thing rather than indulge in an arrogant piece of male chauvinism!

In my experience it is especially difficult for women when you rely on these agencies to give you the right advice. You might have a brilliant idea like the McLaren buggy, but chances are you are going to have to waste a hell of a lot of time, effort and a huge amount of money for very poor-quality advice. There are so many prejudices about women in business and in many other fields that you are going to have to be much better doing your job than your male counterparts. The assumption is that you don't understand finance at all. In my case it was right, because I didn't. But I'm convinced that a lot of the problem lies in the jargon. Accounting terminology immediately strikes terror into many women's brains. As soon as you substitute the various terms and references into something familiar then logic takes over and it all makes sense. But there are a lot of women who do understand finance. They budget their household accounts very effectively. It may be that I'm 46 and out of touch with women who are much younger than me, but I think that the whole ethos of the way that we grew up was that we would not be expected to understand money and that is quite a powerful legacy.

I found an awful lot of people I dealt with in various financial institutions were very uncomfortable dealing with women. If you are assertive you are often seen as butch and overpowering. Unfortunately I would get dreadfully emotional, especially when the business started crashing around my ears, and I would become very impassioned and angry and distressed. I was employing nearly 40 people at that stage and the thought that these wonderfully motivated women, who had gone through so much with us, were being done down through my stupidity, as well as the board's various advisers, was unbearable. My feelings would show and of course that is not the way to run a business. A woman has to understand that in a business world, where men predominate, she shouldn't show her emotions or she will lose her ground.

I was aware that I carried out a 'maternal' style of management, which is now becoming a fashionable way to run a business. I believed then, and I still do, that if you nurture and look after your staff through good and bad times then that will breed loyalty and commitment. I know that in my case the male members of the board saw this as a self-indulgent and namby-pamby way of doing things – a desire to be popular. It had nothing to do with that. It was a much more calculated approach. I could sack people – and did – if it was necessary. But I knew what it was like to work for people and what a huge difference it makes if they respect you. But I do believe that if you want to earn respect you in turn have to respect that person and their role. Also I could see the logic of bringing on people, encouraging people who probably would not have thrived under male management.

A classic example was a woman who worked as an assistant to the person who did the cutting of the clothing. This entailed cutting through about 150 layers of cloth at any one time, amounting to about £4,000 worth of material. She was very reserved and shy and awkward but also steady and patient. We eventually lost the cutter and this woman was left waiting for things to be cut. I suggested to her that she might like to do the cutting herself. Her initial response was 'Who, me? No, I couldn't possibly,' but she did do it. It took her about six weeks to overcome her fear and she was very efficient. Her confidence just blossomed! It was so thrilling to see and she was so proud of herself – and rightly. She never made any mistakes, as the other woman and I had done. She was very accurate, calm and capable. When the business went down she shrank right back and it's such a burden to know that she came out as she did and then went right back in. I do not think she would have succeeded as she did unless someone was prepared to give her a go and I think that that's much more likely to happen where the boss is a woman. I think women are more likely to have that tolerance which goes back to the maternal instinct. After all you don't just write off your kids because they can't spell straight away, you work at it. I think it's similar for a lot of women in business. Also, I think female bosses find it easier than men to recognise that the key people in your business are those at the most menial level, that as a boss I needed them more than they needed me. I think a lot of men have a problem with that.

As we expanded from a small design facility to a full-blown clothing production business we overcame what at times seemed insurmountable hurdles. It was at this time that I was desperately knocking on the development agencies' doors for help with the cost of training. We achieved an exceptionally high standard of training and consequently the workforce was extremely effective. The women were very well motivated. The cost was huge. It was massive. I was keen for my staff to avoid boring repetitive working practices, which are notorious in the clothing industry, and we developed a way of producing the clothing which in effect meant that the women were producing whole garments instead of, say, one sleeve. Working this way as a team was very pleasing. A huge amount of money was consumed in the cost of training – reckoned to be £10,000 to train a standard machinist on a production line. But once we had trained a machinist then more often than not she would stay. Also the clothing itself was quite difficult to make up, so it made sense that the machinists were competent beyond simply banging out a process. This comes back to the 'calculating' approach. I didn't want to see people bored to tears by their work any more than I would have been happy in that situation myself, but equally the standard of work achieved was noticeably better by adopting such an attitude. Although our teething problems had been painful, we gradually got on top of the production side of things.

Marketing, however, was another hurdle. There's always a danger when you're involved with development and production that you lose sight of the main objective, which is that you have got to sell the stuff! It doesn't really matter how brilliant a product it is if it's sitting on a shelf in a warehouse. So often creative people are hopeless when it comes either to selling themselves or even their products. We took advice from a variety of advertising agencies. So many mistakes were made by them as well as by us.

Business failure

Looking back at the whole nightmare I think that the best way of describing it is like having earache and going to the doctor. First of all you do the obvious things, take pills and so on. Initially we did all the things that small businesses do, like gradually building a customer base, achieving a small amount of customer loyalty (which meant repeat sales etc.). We built a fairly respectable mailing list and so on. Then we saw the specialists! We found the result was that, having gone to the doctor with earache, we were being treated for other symptoms. My major crime in this was that I stopped listening to my own instincts. Just like going to a specialist who tells you that it's not your ear that hurts but something quite different, you feel you dare not doubt his judgement and yet your ear goes on hurting.

We were swept along a dizzy trail of statistics and promises – the 'experts' knew, therefore they must be right. We went along with everything they suggested, including the astronomical costs that were incurred as a result. Although the advertising industry is woman-friendly in my experience, this was not the case when it came to questioning their judgement, their advice. I was made to feel an amateur – 'a professional would simply stop probing and get on with it'. Looking back, I don't know whether or not I felt this was a male/female thing. My memory tells me it was, but maybe that's unfair. I do know that I became increasingly concerned and doubtful about the whole relationship.

I think that the biggest difficulty for a woman who's trying to get her point across (certainly this one!) is that often you can become strident. It's very hard to get the balance right and keep faith with yourself. At this stage I had a predominantly male board of directors who had invested in the company – theoretically they had invested in me – but were determined that any major decisions should be made by them. It felt very much like I was a mere woman against this all-male might. I had produced this 'being' – the company – my ideas, conception, whatever. I knew exactly what I wanted for this 'being' but in order to generate growth other people had by then the right to impose their conditions upon that 'being'. In many ways that was a good thing – fresh input, ideas and so on – but every so often the direction would swing wildly away from the main goal and increasingly I was unable to prevent this.

At this stage the growth of the company meant that either 'serious' money had to be invested in it or it could not carry on. We put in every farthing we had. I'd been joined earlier by our investor, who had also sunk a great deal of his own money into the venture. Theoretically it was going to be an ideal working situation – he was going to handle the money side of life while I got on with design, production and sales. After an initial honeymoon period problems began to set in. We clashed. Although theoretically he had joined me in the business in the first place because he liked what I was trying to achieve, my style and my aims, within months he'd tried to change aspects which I felt had to be preserved. Worse, he failed to establish a relationship with my bank manager, who'd been both helpful and supportive. I was appalled as I felt my 'investor', far from smoothing financial waters, had in fact muddied them. It soon became apparent that his motivation and mine differed greatly. While I saw a long-term commitment with hopefully suitable rewards at the end of the day, he saw a short-term turnaround to profit. However, the clothing industry was not going to achieve that for him.

He used his own funds and invested heavily in the business and soon had financial control of the company. At this stage we were still a relatively united board, although it became increasingly confrontational. It may have been the 'investor' was a highly impressionable man. He would only have to meet someone at a dinner party and he would come back with a whole new way of thinking. He vacillated every step of the way. Change would be implemented for change's sake. It may have been that I was simply incapable of putting myself across, but it felt like I was in an echo chamber. Everything I said was bouncing back. I just could not get through to the board, who were in it for something so different. They were in it purely to make money, that was all they were interested in. The reason they became so powerful was that they owned most of the shares. When I started the company it was my business. But we ran out of money, so the 'investor' put more in and with it took more shares out. For a long time I hung on with a tiny majority, but it got too difficult. He said he'd put more money in providing he could retain control, which seemed fair enough. But he became so difficult to deal with that I literally lost my voice – and I have never fully recovered it. This man would turn up at board meetings in London and I'd be unable to speak.

I made one final effort to save the business and approached a venture capital company for investment. They came to see us, liked what they saw and agreed to invest in us. At last we had the kind of money that would take us into a realistic level of production, sales and so on. It meant that the original investors would of course have a much smaller share of 'the cake', but at least we would have a cake. We were able to commit to further advertising on the strength of their involvement but, having agreed to the initial conditions, the 'investor' changed his mind without consulting me – I was the managing director! Realising this, the company withdrew from negotiations and we were left with no money but a very large advertising bill. I didn't know how much all this had to do with my being a woman, but I suspect that the finance director would have been less arrogant with a male managing director.

I knew we couldn't survive after that. We tried every possible way to recover from this disaster for the next six months. My husband and I had allowed our house to be used as a bank guarantee some months before the venture collapsed. However, we ensured that we paid all creditors with the exception of the advertising agency, whom we were unable to pay, and shareholders. We had no choice but to put the company into liquidation. In many ways it was a relief to make such a momentous decision. At least all the indecision was over. But that is when the pain of it started.

The main reasons that the business collapsed were greed and naïveté. The investors were greedy, thinking that a couple of years' work would reap short-term rewards, but you can't look at a small business in that way. On my part, a total lack of experience – utter naïveté. And yet how do you get the experience? You don't get it by working for someone else. You can never get that close. I would adore to be able to get to central government and force them to listen! Able people must be recognised, helped, nurtured. It's ridiculous that as a country we waste such talent and potential. Like education, if you get it right in the early stages, the rest will follow. We must *help* people in the start-up stage – genuine constructive help. It would require an open-mindedness and, above all, a will to see it through. There are an awful lot of us who know how *not* to do something; what we need are the John Harvey Joneses, who make it their business to share their knowledge and flair.

I also think the banks have a huge responsibility. It was a real Jekyll and Hyde situation. One minute they were falling over themselves to lend me money with cups of coffee and first names all round, and then later, when things were not going so well, I'd be shown the door. That made me feel almost like a criminal. I didn't want it to be like that, I did not deliberately put my family in jeopardy – I just got it wrong. Obviously the recession had a huge part to play in it as well. But I do think the banks in this country fail to appreciate the intelligence of equipping their own people with a bit of business experience. Apparently, if you borrow money from a bank in Germany, not only are you asked to produce a business plan, as you are here, but often the bank appoints someone to see your business in operation, sitting in on the odd board meeting and so on, so that not only will the bank employee know about your business but he or she will be gaining in valuable experience themselves in the world of business. At the moment a lot of the business advisers and banks have no experience outside banking. By definition they can't know what it's like in the 'real world'. They have relatively secure jobs, subsidised (bank) mortgages, and risk is the ultimate four-letter word!

So many people suffered as a result of my business collapsing. We didn't manage to pay the advertising agency, the staff were laid off, and many of them haven't been able to find a job. The 'investor' lost a staggering amount of money and my husband and I lost the lot! It took us two years to sell our house for £70,000 less than we had paid for it. We are currently living in a mobile home with two teenage children, both of whom are at each other's throats all the time. It's an absolute nightmare. We also have two dogs. Mercifully the hamster kicked up his heels a couple of months ago! I see people with whom I had worked struggle to maintain a basic standard of living. The waste is wicked, the guilt is overwhelming.

The effect of all this on me and my family has been devastating. Losing the business is a similar experience to bereavement. I'm conscious that it may sound banal to talk in these terms, but losing the business really was like a death. It was something we really cared about and the feelings of helplessness as it gradually drifted away were absolute agony. When the business went down there were all the financial horrors – things like the fact that over 30 people had been put out of work and we had to see them every day, especially those who had been with me from the start. One woman was left practically destitute because her husband went bankrupt. That was particularly grim. The guilt was overpowering. My husband was – and still is to some extent – angry about the whole thing. He joined the board at a rather late stage and I felt he was manipulated by the other members. It was also quite demoralising for him, as he wasn't being paid anything. The other board members would say things like, 'Well, if you want to put your wife out of business ...' It was a crazy time. One minute we were working amicably together, the next we'd be screeching at each other. It was difficult working together because of all the tension.

The feeling of loss has been overwhelming. On top of all that the financial problems seem to duplicate yearly! Four years after liquidation we still owe money and the nightmare continues. I sometimes can't believe it has all happened. I had never known fear and despair could be like this.

The whole situation placed a fantastic strain on our marriage. My business failing financially ruined my husband – it's as simple as that. We have had to deal with emotions which often couldn't be expressed – just dealing with the realities of what's happened is difficult enough. The children have also had a distressing and confusing time of it all. I long to be able to repair the damage. I couldn't believe that losing our business and our home had all happened as a direct result of what I had done.

My husband and I found that we couldn't be there for each other. Part of me was guilt-ridden and the other part was bloody furious. I wanted to shake him and say, 'Enough! We have done this number!' I wanted to let go of it much earlier than he did. I found it terribly difficult that he couldn't forgive. He said he couldn't be expected to agree with everything I said. I think he felt extremely frightened by the way things were going and he was fed up and angry and no matter what I said he would disagree with it. Nevertheless it hurt. Obviously this permeated our private lives as well and that was very difficult too. We couldn't agree on anything – not even what to eat for dinner! I know I argue passionately about things I care about. I think a lot of women do, whereas men will often argue for the sake of it.

It has affected us profoundly as a couple. Outwardly we probably appeared fine, but in private we were two totally separate, isolated people. I'm still not sure that we are through it or whether we've managed so far through habit or a deep understanding between us. There have been lots of things that have kept us together. Although I was bloody angry with him at times I also felt very sorry for him and the way the business went. It's difficult enough for a man to leave his profession anyway, but to come into this kind of chaos and into a very female environment as well can't have been easy for him.

My relationship with my two daughters was also extremely difficult. I felt that as a working mother I was at least accessible. The factory building was near our house, but they remember my being too busy to be there to give them their supper and so on. I was certainly there for them when they were very little and, although they say I was not there when they were older, I'm sure I was, although I'm not an earth mother type. The kids had lots of problems around the fact that I wasn't a conventional mother. Also I was an employer in the area and most of the kids of my employees went to the same school as mine. I remember one mother who didn't get a job with us and the kids came in for a bit of flak at school. Also our house was very large and overlooked the back of the school, so they were often ribbed about being 'posh'. On the other hand they have grown up in a very creative environment and both have benefited from that.

It took me a long time to unscramble the effects of the business. The anger was overpowering. The worry affected me physically – especially my voice. At one point I had no voice at all. I'm an asthmatic and that got worse. I also got extremely fat. I just pigged out. All the things that make you feel more rotten. But it was instant gratification. For a long time I couldn't stop looking over my shoulder. I couldn't let it go. I am sure my friends were sick of me. I went on and on. It felt so strange. I no longer had the business. There was the public face and trying to make things normal for the kids, not wanting them to experience a completely different standard of living from what they had been used to. All or nothing – no income.

Alongside all this I have also experienced kindness and support: having been extremely critical of development agencies, one source of inspiration is a man who works for a business centre locally who recently ran a course which was both relevant and constructive. I just wish that he were not such a lone voice. The general approach hasn't changed all that much, I suspect. Lots of other people have also been great and it's been a very maturing experience!

Do I regret what has happened? Wholeheartedly. I see failure as a huge burden of responsibility. My one aim in life is to attempt to undo some of the harm I've done. I am also a born optimist. Even when things are at their most grim I'm conscious that I've learned so much. I just wish to God that it had not been at such a cost to other people.

Business failure

The first couple of years since the business collapsed have passed by in a sort of haze. It took me some time to make my head work again! About eighteen months ago I realised that I was thinking differently in terms of what I want to achieve. I do want to go back into the business I know and love – clothing – but from a totally different viewpoint. Having always been a manufacturer's designer (I think of garments in terms of production lines and so on) I'm now aware that I'm very much more in tune with the customer than I was before. Throughout this period of time, which has forced me away from the production end, I've been staggered by just how difficult buying clothes is for many British women. I've gone through my self-imposed exile – a sort of guilt quarantine. I don't think having failed means that you forfeit the right to try to get it right, although I did at first because of the guilt. I now feel that the opposite is the case. If you can't learn by mistakes, then where or how can you learn? I am no longer that naïve person I was ten years ago. I know that in many ways I'll never be as confident as I was before. I am certainly a lot more cautious. Again using driving as an example, it's as if I've had a major pile-up, written off a much-loved car, but I'm now a safer driver. I'm taking stock now and attempting to get back into that driving seat – all without a penny.

For further details see Chapter 15. Business debts; and Chapter 17. Bankruptcy: three women's experiences.

JOSEPHINE: BANKRUPTCY, REPOSSESSION AND SURVIVAL

Josephine considers herself very lucky. So does her solicitor. He said that she was the luckiest person he knew. She and her partner had put their house up as collateral should their business fail. It did fail and the bank wanted to sell their house as per the agreement.

Josephine was lucky in that a very similar case had been heard in the House of Lords while her case was being negotiated. This other couple's success lay in their proving that the bank had not adequately ensured at the time of the loan that they had fully understood the implications and consequences of using their house as collateral against business failure. Largely as a direct result of this case, Josephine was able to keep her half of the house and buy out her partner's share – which the bank eventually claimed as collateral – after several years of fear, anguish and uncertainty that reminded her of her childhood fear of losing her house in the war through bombing. Alongside this she tried to maintain a positive attitude through meditation.

Although she rather resented the notion that women do not fully understand business, in this case not only was it true but thankfully so.

My partner and I got into financial difficulties over his design business. It was shortly before the recession and the philosophy at the time was 'you have got to expand, got to expand'. Banks were very easy about lending money. We wanted to update our equipment and the bank readily agreed. All we needed was to put the house up as collateral. Keith and I owned the house jointly and we signed the necessary forms. It was the late 1970s. Looking back, we were not actually borrowing very much although it felt like a lot at the time. The business was very successful and it was a wonderful atmosphere to work in. Quite a number of others were going under in the mini-recession of the late 1970s but we were doing well. We were small and efficient and interestingly enough almost everyone who worked there meditated. It was a wonderful atmosphere to work in.

As we became more successful we got bigger and we had to employ more people. I was actively involved in running the business but decided to leave in the mid-1980s to do homoeopathy training. In many ways I was disconnected from the business. I didn't really pay much attention to details like how the business was doing – especially when it was doing well – unless there was a dramatic change. I just trundled on. Perhaps it's a cultural thing – I'd been brought up to believe that this was the way a woman should behave and not bother herself with the business side of things.

The recession bit deeper and there were also other problems. There were more problems with staff, with the need to update equipment. Being successful was in some ways quite difficult to keep going. The reason we finally went into receivership was that we had too many bad debts – too many people who were not paying up. Some had gone bust themselves. Some would complain about the work, saying there was something wrong with it, which was often questionable but meant they didn't pay what they owed.

I think Keith started to feel exhausted with the business and lost interest in it after nearly twenty years. The debts had increased from around £10,000 to £120,000 and as the financial climate worsened the bank got more demanding. The last few years were a huge struggle for survival. We lurched from one job to another and it became increasingly precarious. There was also the possibility that if the business went down we might also lose the house – to the bank. It was always in the back of my mind. At times we thought that if we went into liquidation we may be able to save the house. But there was also the feeling that if we invested a bit more and got over this hump we'd be OK. And so the debts increased.

I didn't blame Keith. He was the one with the expertise. I knew nothing whatsoever about design or running a business. I needed to leave because I didn't want to spend my time being a receptionist. It was very interesting for a while but I wanted to do other things. I tended to discount my value in the business partly because I saw it as a fairly low-value job. I didn't know anything about commercial design and I didn't particularly want to learn about it. It was only when we got a replacement that she pointed out that I wasn't paying an insurance stamp. In fact I wasn't even paid a salary. We just lived off the proceeds. I hadn't thought about it until then. In hindsight I can't believe that I was so naïve. I just was! My pay was so low that I didn't pay any tax on it. It slowly dawned on me that when I wanted to buy something I would have to ask Keith. I also realised that I didn't like it. I think it only really sank home after I left the business and started earning a little money of my own.

It's hard for me looking back to see how much our relationship was affected by our financial ties, especially when I left the business to study and was wanting to make personal changes. It's difficult to say what aspects were affected by what and whether they were attributable to the usual sorts of negotiations that couples need to make from time to time – or not; and how much was due to our business and personal relationship getting out of sync or whether the relationship triggered something negative in the business.

After I left the business and started my homoeopathy training my life changed greatly. It was hard, partly because it was so expensive to do the training. Typically I didn't sit down and think, 'how much is this going to cost me?' If I had, I probably wouldn't have done it. Nor did I think of myself as a career woman who earned money. Although I'd finished my Open University studying and I also had a degree in psychology from years ago I hadn't ever had a career. I'd just been someone who'd been married and had children. I originally trained as a teacher. I did an English degree in my twenties. I had a job as a teacher for a couple of years and then got married and lived abroad and didn't really work after that – apart from doing voluntary work teaching English – until the children grew up.

I'd been brought up to believe that women really belonged in the home. Women didn't need to work. But I think that throughout the whole of my married life there was always a sense of needing to get out and do something for me but I couldn't or didn't manage to do that. There was partly a sense of frustration of what am I going to do with my life? Also that my needs always felt as if they were secondary to my partner's – particularly when my children were born. There was also a degree of relief that at least I didn't have to think about work for a while. I never, ever thought I'd be involved in a design business – albeit a very high quality design business. Although I enjoyed it I would never have dreamt of it as being something I would like to do.

Although I was doing my homoeopathy training – and it was what I wanted to do – I felt very powerless. I didn't feel confident enough with the experience I'd acquired to work and to use it. In addition the business was beginning to falter and my security was being threatened. The business had enabled me to study and had meant that I didn't have to pay rent. It was solely because the business was in operation that I could afford to go and do my training. We were beginning to get into troubled waters and it was something that neither of us could've foreseen. This all happened very gradually but as the business became more precarious I became increasingly anxious. So did Keith. I think in part that it was responsible for what happened to us and our relationship, although it's always hard to know what has triggered what. I think we failed to tackle our own anxieties. Also we weren't working together any more so we didn't have that kind of contact. We both laboured under the assumption that it was all going to be all right. We believed it would be, although I was anxious about it. One of our major differences was that he tended to be much more optimistic than me. He would keep reassuring me that it was going to be OK.

My main anxiety was that we were going to lose the house and that I'd have nowhere to live. Also I wouldn't have the earning capacity to support myself. My children were in their teens and still at school. In some ways I wasn't so anxious about them because their father would've helped out. They wouldn't have become homeless. I was also feeling very uncertain at that time about who I was and where I was going. It felt like I'd taken a very big step. I've no idea how different the training might've been if I'd been financially secure. I don't know to what degree my identity was mixed up in the uncertainty of material things and psychological things.

I think I resisted being anxious as best I could. One of the manifestations of this was that I did work extremely hard. I often took on work that I didn't want to do like running workshops because I needed the money. I didn't always feel comfortable with some of this work because I wasn't always confident that I was experienced enough to do it, especially running groups. But if there was an opportunity to make money I had to take it. I became focused on how I could earn money in a way that I'd never in my life considered. So one of my main things was make money, make money. It was 'be strong' and 'work hard'.

I think that I carried the anxiety for both of us. I don't think that Keith was all that anxious, at least that's how it felt to me. He's the sort of person who focuses very successfully on the here and now. He doesn't waste a lot of time thinking up what awful things might happen. I agree with his attitude that worrying about it isn't going to solve the problem. It's best to get on and do something. And far more appropriate. I think I was anxious partly because I'm getting older and partly because I have moved around a lot in my life and I'd got to a point where I wanted to stay for a while. It was the first time I had ever regarded my house as a home. I'd made a big investment in it – I'd put a lot of 'myself' into it.

My main feeling was fear. One of the good things at the time was that I had a lot of support around me on my course. There were no straight answers to my cries for help except advice about not making assumptions that the worst was going to happen. I was born during the war and it was a bit like having one's house bombed. So it was almost like a childhood fear – except that it was probably everyone's fear during the war. It certainly was my mother's fear and it was a very understandable one as houses were being bombed. I don't actually recollect as a small child fearing the house would be bombed but I remember having to go into the air-raid shelter and so on. So I can speculate a connection with a very early childhood fear of the possibility of losing my home to the present-day home which felt like a bomb was going to drop out of the sky and demolish it.

I felt like that for about three years before the business went into liquidation and then there was the assumption that the 'bomb' had dropped; that was followed by a period of feeling helpless – what do I do now? This was followed by more than two years fighting the bank over whether or not the bank had a legal right to hold us to our 'agreement' over the house.

The solicitor I saw was fantastic. He fought the bank really hard for me. I'd been to see him about three years before we went into liquidation because I was getting desperate. I needed somewhere to live and work from as a homoeopath as I still wasn't earning enough money to support myself and pay rent on a house and workplace. I'd found a flat which seemed reasonable and went to see this solicitor. I didn't tell anyone that I'd gone. I wanted to know if there was any way that I could get out of the agreement with the bank. He didn't think that I could extricate myself completely but said that I might have a chance of avoiding being held responsible for some of the debts because we weren't married. He reckoned that if we had been married we would've been equally responsible and I wouldn't have a hope in hell. As it was, there was a glimmer of hope in that I mightn't be totally liable for every single debt. But it seemed that all I could really do was to sit it out and wait and hope that the business would survive.

He advised me not to move out of my house. He then looked into the situation and found that the piece of paper I had signed all those years ago regarding the house was not valid in that the bank had not properly discharged their duty to me as they had failed to explain fully the implications should the business fail.

There was a similar case around at the same time that had been given a lot of publicity. A woman owed the bank a large amount of money because of a business failure where her house had been put up as collateral. Her solicitor claimed that she was not aware of the implications of this 'deal' and that the bank had failed in its duty to properly inform her of the consequences of using her house as collateral. She appealed and it went to the House of Lords who found in her favour. I remember hearing it on the news on my car radio and cheering. I'm sure it affected my case.

My solicitor's wranglings with the bank went on for about two and a half years because initially the bank said 'nonsense'. It was very protracted and complicated and there were wrangles over which part of the business I did own. My solicitor took a

Business failure

considerable amount of pleasure in fighting the bank. But I suppose I did ultimately benefit from the notion or 'culture' that women do not easily understand these things – which in my case was true.

I still hadn't completed my training at this point and the thing that I found most difficult to do while all this was going on was to study – or to write anything creative. I'd flung myself into working as a way of coping but I was unable to sit down and do any work for my exams. I actually felt that I was incapable of doing it. It was like it was an existence issue that was about just keeping going – not about working on a case study. I could be creative in other ways, just not creative when it came to studying.

What I needed to do was to empower myself as much as I could and one of the things I could do was to envisage a positive future. One image was to see myself staying in the house although my future there was totally unknown. I'd also go round looking at properties in estate agents' windows and thinking that I could afford those. I'd visualise myself as being able to live in that place. Also I didn't want to dwell on it being the worst possible scenario. I needed to do a lot of soul-searching and asking myself what I wanted in life. It was part of my developing strategy for coping with what was happening. I also meditated.

I became much more positive. It may've been partly due to the fact that once Keith moved out I didn't have the anxiety and tension of living with somebody. It was easier to deal with this whole situation on my own than trying to work within what was becoming an increasingly uneasy relationship. In some ways it was a relief. I had more energy as it wasn't going into trying to sort out a relationship as well as everything else. I suppose that'd be rather a feminine thing to do and feel responsible for one's partner being unhappy. I felt responsible for Keith feeling unhappy – but not for the distress he later felt at the business going down. But I also felt useless when it came to trying to make things better and I was aware that I wasn't very good at it.

I think that for most of my life I've been pretty casual about things. One of the changes of this sort of experience for me was that, against my inclination, I felt that I couldn't afford to be casual any more and I had to take things seriously. And yet I know I can still think, 'Oh, what the hell! I want that so I'm going to get it.'

Looking back on this experience – and the debt which was well over £100,000 – I don't think that I perceived myself as being in debt. I didn't feel that I owed money. Perhaps I thought that if anybody owed it, it wasn't me. It was the firm or the business. I didn't have any moral feelings about the bank. (It was the bank that was calling in the house.) I thought that if anyone owed the money I suppose it was Keith, although it wasn't as cut and dried as that. I know I didn't feel guilt in terms of the money. But I felt as though perhaps I'd been a failure in other ways in terms of the relationship and how we'd negotiated this whole period. I also felt a failure in terms of not being able to support myself. That was very difficult because although I had to learn how to do things quickly – in terms of my job – I also felt very uncomfortable doing it. Some of it was painful but some of it was very good. It also meant that I did a lot of things that I mightn't normally have done – or felt. I was invited to do some teaching and my immediate reaction would've been not to feel confident or skilled enough. But I went ahead and did things like that in spite of my feelings. I remember on that occasion doing an enormous amount of work for the course and feeling terribly anxious, but I got through it. I told myself that I mustn't turn these opportunities down, that I must go forward, that I needed the experience. I knew at the time that my anxiety was fuelling the need to learn.

It's interesting looking at meditation in all of this because it's as if it has come full circle. It kind of fits in at the beginning when I first met Keith and had recently learnt to meditate. I became a bit guarded with this type of meditation, was not sure where I was going with it and felt it was a bit chauvinistic. Over the years I kept up meditating but also slightly letting it go. Years later I was introduced to another more relaxed type of meditation where the philosophy was rather different and more interesting although I was still not 'sure' about it. For some reason I kept going back to the workshops and kept going with meditation. The teacher's message, as I understood it, was 'OK, so it does not matter if you do not believe it. Just do it. Meditate on a good outcome – the outcome you want.' So I did actually meditate quite a lot on getting the house – on being able to keep my half and to be able to afford to buy Keith's share from the bank. I'm not sure that I really believed it. But slowly, slowly it began to look as though there was a glimmer of hope and that I just might get it. This went on becoming more and more possible; right up until the very last month there was no means of knowing if I would even be able to afford it, should I be offered it. As it got nearer to completion there was a point when I thought that the bank might settle for £70,000 which would be cheap – even though I didn't have the money to get it. But could I afford to let it go? That would have been the ultimate irony, to have missed out!

It was this period in particular that affected my health, especially my sleep. I'd never had insomnia before and I was having lots of nights with consistently very little sleep. It got to the stage where I would wonder every night whether or not I'd get to sleep. I think it was because of the ultimate uncertainty of everything. Although it was becoming increasingly likely that there was a chance that I might be offered the house, there was also the uncertainty about what figure the bank would want for it. I had no control over it.

Keith and I didn't officially agree to separate and still saw each other from time to time. He eventually gave up the job he'd been head-hunted for after the business folded and went and did whatever he felt like. He thoroughly enjoyed himself. He's now a free agent. In some ways I found it quite inspiring. It opened up possibilities for me as well. There was no question that he was going to give me any money – even though he was going to be earning a good salary.

I'm not sure how all this affected my relationship with my children. They had both left home by the time it happened so they were less directly affected by it than they might otherwise have been. Obviously my state of mind would've had an influence but I would like to think it's not had too much of a negative effect on them. They knew what was going on but I tended not to express too much. They knew that I was upset from time to time but I was also doing other things and they could see that.

In the end I got the house back – or at least I was able to buy Keith's half from the bank for a small amount of money. We went into voluntary liquidation after the bank instructed us to sell the house and then informed the receivers that we were doing so. My solicitor throughout all of this was quite amazing. I think he just went on and on at the bank, telling them that this was what they were going to do. Afterwards he said: 'You are one of the luckiest people I've ever met.' He'd been reassuring me all along but at the end said he never thought we would do it! He was definitely the right man for the job and yet a number of people said they thought I should get another solicitor.

My advice to other women in the same position as me is 'don't do it'. Do not be prepared to put up your house as a guarantee should a business venture fail. At the time it may seem to be the only way to expand a business. There are other ways. You need to know exactly what the situation is, what the risks are. If you are doing it through a bank they now have to be seen to be doing their duty by giving you all the facts about the risks and so on. They now have their own solicitor present. My advice is to make sure you *really do understand all the information*, the situation and the risks attached. It can sometimes be intimidating having all these people present with documents to read and sign but it is vital that you do understand it all.

The worst time for me throughout all of this was feeling as though I had no future – or no acceptable future. What I had to do was to say that I did have a future – and that I could see ways in which that future could evolve that were acceptable and believable.

There is life after repossession. By the time I actually got the house, I knew I was going to survive anyway. Also there were amazing opportunities that came along at that time that I wouldn't have believed possible. A lot of my experience was about a struggle to find my own identity and survival.

For further details see Chapter 15. Business debts; and Chapter 17. Bankruptcy: three women's experiences.

5 Personal addictions

MARGARET: HEROIN, MOTHERHOOD AND ABSTINENCE

Margaret first tried heroin in 1975 after she lost her young son in a drowning accident. She discovered it was useful to block out her feelings. Before this happened she had been quite a successful business woman with her own record promotion company. She had a lot of money and she spent it all. She had been a teenager in the 1960s and loved her freedom, but at the same time she depended on a man for happiness.

Margaret became increasingly dependent on heroin. At first she could manage her habit as she was earning good money and using only occasionally. Gradually she became more and more dependent on it. She lost her job because of it and this was the start of a downward spiral of debt, despair and drug abuse.

Heroin had been useful as a means of not getting close to people. It was only when Margaret fell in love and wanted to get in touch with her feelings that she decided to come off it. Her partner was also an addict. This was the beginning of a ten-year battle with heroin, methadone and alcohol, during which time they had two children.

Margaret is one of the 37,164 notified addicts registered in the UK in 1995; of these 24,500 are registered heroin addicts like Margaret. In addition there are almost 17,500 who are registered methadone users and about 3,000 registered cocaine users. Workers in the field reckon that for every one addict registered there are at least five addicts who are not. The increase of drug use and abuse is reflected in the Home Office Bulletin figures: in 1991 there were 20,000 notified addicts and this figure almost doubled in the following five years. Drugs are much more widely available throughout the UK than ever before and their use has increased dramatically.

I am 44. I've recently noticed how I've followed a pattern in my life. I've been married twice – once when I was 19 and again when

I was 34. Before I married I had my own company promoting records and I also worked for different record and management companies. I had money, lots of money, and I spent it all. I have this thing between money and happiness – the desire to be happy and realising that money does not fulfil that in any way whatsoever. And I married someone who wasn't well off. I'd had a couple of proposals from millionaires but I didn't love them. Instead I chose a recently qualified engineer who seemed a safe bet in terms of a happy family situation. I had a long-term vision of being comfortable with him and not worrying about money, settling down and having 2.4 children and going to Sainsbury's on Fridays.

It was a completely different lifestyle from the one I'd been living. One part of me had the message to be successful and to be myself. That was from the '60s – the fact that I could be free to be myself and I didn't need a man to look after me, but part of me still thought that happiness came by being with a man. I had the two messages at once: the freedom of the '60s and the burning of the bras which I thought was brilliant, but I still had the message from my childhood and other influences like the media that you married somebody you loved and lived happily ever after. It was a very childlike sort of thinking.

My first marriage was also my first experience of debt and how things don't work out quite as you hoped. I persuaded myself that I was in love with my husband. Shortly after we were married, he stopped working for about a year. I'd been looking to him to provide in the financial sense, to reinstate my ideal, and my parents had been pushing in the background and eventually he started to work again. I've absolutely no idea why he stopped working. I had known him for over a year before we married, when he was one kind of person, and after we married he became someone else overnight. I suppose that, looking back, the same could be said of me because I was a successful business woman who had her own company and was never short of money, and when we married I stopped working too. So we both did exactly the same thing which is a complete recipe for disaster when it comes to providing and having 2.4 children. We didn't even talk about it! It just happened. I got pregnant, which was part of my recipe for happiness – marriage and children and that I would be the wife at home cleaning things and looking after the little baby and he'd be out there earning loads of money and we would be very happy and go for holidays. None of that happened. We stayed with my parents for the first year and pushed to get a place from the local council. My father did lots of lying, saying that we could only use the kitchen and bathroom at certain times, and when my son was a year old we were given a council flat.

I never knew how much my husband earned. I thought I did but in truth I don't think I did. I scratched about for more cash and worked part-time for my father and took my son with me for about three hours a day. I used that money to buy food. We were so short of money I gave up smoking as there was not enough money for food and everything else. I fed my husband and my child and ate the leftovers and felt thoroughly depressed and miserable and at the grand old age of 21 was wondering what had happened and why it was not going right. I was also wanting to help him find a future work-wise. Eventually he got a job in the Middle East fixing helicopters. He was given a family villa and I thought we were back on track, ex-pats, earning loads of money with nothing to do in the middle of nowhere. Off we went but his earnings were not all that large and there wasn't anything left over. I spent a lot on phone calls home.

I only stayed eight months. My husband's behaviour deteriorated into something bordering on psychopathic. One moment he'd be expansive, warm, generous and normal and the next he'd be completely violent and raging mad and do scary things to me. He beat the hell out of me in front of Patrick, our little boy, and would not stop – even though I was bleeding all over the bathroom floor and trying to protect Patrick. So that was it. It was one time too many and I decided to go home. It took about a month to get it all organised. He ripped up my passport and set fire to it, rubbed it in my face and flushed the bits down the toilet. I had to get a replacement. I left my clothes and tickets at a friend's place. I didn't tell anyone, though. I was too proud. He eventually realised I wasn't coming back and refused to give me my possessions. I never saw them again.

I moved back in with my parents. They helped me financially to do a secretarial qualification which was virtually the only kind of work available to mothers who have children at school – unless you want to work in a factory. Then Patrick, my little son, drowned. It changed everything. I had no one to look after any more. I didn't need to work part-time any more. I was in complete shock and completely numb and unable to talk about it. I missed out the grieving bit altogether. I couldn't move towards it in the slightest. My parents got me to see a psychiatrist straight away and

I found him a waste of time. My mother told me I came back saying, 'He's not helping me. All he does is to keep asking me questions and then telling me that I know the answers.' I stopped seeing him and went back to work.

I found another job in the music industry. I was back to what I knew – answering to myself and for myself but I had not quite made the break from home. I would leave for a few months and go back. It was only a few miles from the centre of London. My mother had a weird way with money. I expected to pay for my keep and I'd ask her how much she wanted and she'd tell me to keep it as I wasn't earning very much. Then it became, 'If you give so much then I'll save it for you and give it back to you when you really need it.' But I didn't bother with that as it seemed a bit pointless. I needed it now. I was only 25 and thought the future would be taken care of – that one day I would meet this man who would be well-established with everything and I would just fit into that slot, because that's how I would be happy. I just bought the old ideals about men, although part of me wanted autonomy and independence.

The year my son died, 1975, was the year I tried heroin for the first time. I had a series of disastrous relationships that came and went and I decided that I was the sort of woman who was better off not having long-term relationships. Also I didn't want to have any more children. I thought it would be better not to get close to anyone because it was so painful and full of angst. If I felt really stressed, hurt, upset or miserable I could use a bit of heroin and feel better. I would use it like that and at times not use it because I was fulfilling myself at work. I had status at work – I was somebody – so I didn't always need to use heroin. I used it in that way until the beginning of the 1980s when I was more emotionally upset and used it more often. I moved from using it occasionally, like once a week or on the odd occasion, to having some handy all the time. It'd take a week or so to be addicted to it physically and the same time to stop. Stopping was like recovering from the flu – sneezing, coughing, aching, weak – in its mildest form. So this was how I lived – always 'catching' the flu. I think that's what I really believed – it was flu and not withdrawal symptoms.

I was spending about £50 a week at that time which was manageable given what I was earning. I also used cocaine then which is very good for (false) self-esteem. One becomes chemically empowered – one can walk on water, do anything. I found a good source that I could buy large quantities from and then sell it on to friends which would easily pay for my cocaine. I made lots of money that way and it was the only time in my life when I've managed to save. I had too much money so I had to put some in the bank. In fact I had £700 just sitting in the bank. When I realised that I spent it.

I was made a director of the company I was working for; I had been head-hunted for that job. I ran music tours that went all over the world. All my expenses were paid for by the company on credit cards and I was given a company car. My habit also came out of the business. It was great having anything I wanted. It made me feel very secure – like that's how it ought to be, not having to worry about where the next penny was coming from and being supported by finance. I didn't need huge amounts. I didn't go mad and rush off and buy Gucci shoes. I felt really supported and secure which was the feeling that was lacking in my personal life. I was saving money too – but that was unintentional.

My parents hadn't taught me how to save. They'd been quite hard up for most of my childhood. There was a scarcity about things where finances were concerned. When my father was able, he put money by for me in the form of insurances and endowments and saved for me that way. But I eventually cashed them all in because it seemed too long to wait. I picked up the scarcity feeling but when I was working I felt supported and the need to save didn't arise. What I learnt to do was to borrow when I needed to and to pay it back.

But my well-paid job and my security didn't last. The owner of the company sold off some of the assets and closed it down. He went off to America. I went too. I stayed with family friends in New York and we 'looked after' huge amounts of cocaine that came from South America. I also worked as an accountant and paid for my board – just like I should've done with my parents. When I stopped working I was living there in the same way as I did with my parents – with the unspoken expectation that these family friends were now my parents and they were paying for my life and looking after me. They got fed up with that, understandably, so I flew off to Dallas and worked as a waitress for a while. I still had my credit cards which I used and abused – upping my credit limits and things. Eventually I realised that it was all going to come to an end – the job, the credit cards, the lot – so I bought a ticket, went skiing, then returned to England, to my parents.

I got another job in the music industry with some very nice people and was determined to sort things out. I was working like other people, had a boss and was getting a wage. It was a far cry from what I had been used to. I did their books. They were managing a very successful band overseas and the band earned lots of money. I could write myself cheques and lose it creatively. I stole loads of money from them to support my heroin habit which by now really was a habit and I couldn't do without it. It was now my security and costing at least £50 a day which was more than I was earning. It was awful. I couldn't help myself doing it and I couldn't live easily with myself having done it – which meant I needed the heroin even more to get rid of all those feelings. So then I needed more! Having given myself permission to do it once, it then became very regular and then completely out of hand. One day I lost a packet of heroin in the office. I couldn't find it anywhere. The next day the office manager had found it and said it was mine and that I had better leave. So I did.

By that time I had met this man John who is now my second husband and suddenly, for the first time in my life, I wanted to be happy. I wanted that more than anything else. I wanted to experience the happiness that I knew was around us but that I couldn't get into. I went to a private clinic to come off the heroin and John tried to do the same at home, but it didn't work for him – and I was only successful for a couple of months. This was 1985. The same thing happened as happened when I first got married. John was a heroin dealer making money and I had my ways of making enough to support me, and together we imagined that that would blossom. In fact it made it twice as bad because we were in debt all the time, unable to buy food from supermarkets and that sort of thing.

I began to sign on – to buy into that downtrodden, deprived package that it is. The place where I signed on was full of anger and had beer cans on the floor and women with pushchairs and snotty-nosed babies. It was like 'this is my life' because my self-worth was so low from stealing that money and all the rest of it. My husband was already registered as an addict and he suggested that I do the same, which meant that I couldn't keep it a secret any more – the whole world would know. I registered because there was nothing else I could do. John and I together couldn't support our habit so I began to get methadone scripts to help me come off the heroin. I didn't have any confidence left to go out to work as an autonomous being and I didn't feel I had the necessary skills to do very much. I did have some skills but no sense of self-worth to go out and do something positive because I'd done such awful things to get money to support my habit and I couldn't stop using. I couldn't stop myself. I tried. I tried methadone scripts short-term and out-patients and going for counselling. They offered support but they were powerless to help me because I couldn't help myself. I was powerless over my habit. It was very depressing. Eventually I was able to get agency work as a secretary. Sometimes I was using heroin, sometimes I wasn't because I would have just come off a methadone script. I wasn't getting much money but what I earned we used for food. We got a flat but there never seemed to be enough left over to pay the rent. We were living in London and got this flat through my parents. We were able to pay a lump sum occasionally if John was dealing but usually it was spent on other things – necessities like heroin or alcohol and food, in that order. The less heroin we used the more methadone scripts we tried and the further away we got, the more we started drinking.

Heroin was £80 a gramme and over the next six years it went up to £120, then down to £100 then back to £120. It also depended where we got it from. A gramme lasted for as long as it took to use it. It could be hours. We would have, say, half a gramme each and that would last for a period of 24 hours. I was getting £30 something a week in benefit. John was still dealing so we always had heroin there and when we came off it – when we were on the methadone and not buying it – he would not need to deal and we could live off the money we were getting, more or less. We tried coming off heroin for six and a half years by using methadone.

Falling in love was the one thing that kept me persevering. It was important so I could feel the happiness. It took a long time. Then I got pregnant with my daughter in 1987 and rapidly weaned myself off. We were having a lot of arguments. It was a very tense time. I was determined. We were really looking forward to having our daughter. We already knew the sex before she was born. My son had drowned and I had a real need to know if this was a replacement son or something entirely different like a daughter! We felt very supported by Kings College Hospital and told them everything about our drugs and so on. We both thought the baby's life was more important than keeping secrets. Their support helped me with my determination not to use again while I was pregnant. But the moment I started having contractions I had to send John out for some heroin because I knew it was going to hurt.

We continued trying to come off heroin altogether for several more years after our daughter was born. We would try to distance ourselves from the heroin by taking methadone and then wean ourselves off the methadone in the hope that things would be all right. I suppose we could've gone to Narcotics Anonymous but I saw the word 'God' in one of their leaflets and I was still angry with God for drowning my son. One good thing about the heroin was that it did help me to go over what had happened. When I was sufficiently narcotically numb I could bring the whole thing up into my awareness and go over it and feel the feelings which were really excruciating regardless of what I was using. I could allow the feelings to come up because they didn't overwhelm me. But I couldn't do it without the heroin.

With my not working I was relying on maternity grants but it was all so little! And it never arrived on time. I got the grant for my maternity clothes two months after she was born! It was always 'in hand'. I was trying to live on that small amount of money and face a future that was unknown – and I was determined not to go back on heroin because that would make it worse. I didn't want my daughter to be affected in any way by the behaviour that goes with heroin. It didn't work all that well, so a few months after her birth we moved in with my parents – again!

We were both looking for work and using heroin on and off. We would've been taken to court by our landlord for a huge sum of money that we still owed. We talked him down to half and my parents paid it so we didn't go to court. I didn't have credit cards any more and the debts had been written off by a very kindly solicitor whom I saw privately. I don't know how he did it. It was a miracle. I had run up thousands of pounds on my credit cards. I couldn't have paid them off anyway.

John found a job as a trainee warehouse manager and I found a job as a caretaker looking after seven blocks of flats for a Housing Association. Accommodation was included. My mother looked after the baby all day while I worked and John went out to his job. So here we were. A family providing for itself! That included a bit of help from my parents. We still had the same story – sometimes methadone, sometimes heroin, sometimes nothing, loads of drink . . . that lasted until I couldn't hack my job any more. It was a job for two people but I was doing it on my own. I really wasn't fit or capable of doing it anyway. I resigned and they moved us to a council flat. John carried on working and I stayed at home. I got pregnant with my little boy and I think I got post-natal depression instantly. I just couldn't stop using heroin – or I couldn't stop drinking – and it felt like there was no way out. It was getting dangerous – for all of us. How could I provide a future for them? My idea was to keep him away from me and then he wouldn't pick any of this up.

We followed the same financial pattern as we always did: we didn't have enough money to pay the rent although mostly we got Housing Benefit so it was paid direct. We'd bought a car on an HP agreement when we were both working and had a bank account. My mother had given us her car but that was falling to bits due to our dysfunctional driving. Both sides had been caved in – on my way to get heroin. I knew how to buy a new one – not by saving up but through a loan. We had a bank account, a bank loan and our credit was OK. So we created a debt to pay back which of course we were unable to do when I got pregnant and stopped working. Also we were using heroin again because things were so desperately miserable. I tried very hard not to use while I was pregnant and in the end managed to avoid it by sleeping. So I spent the latter half of my pregnancy asleep. It was safest. I used to sleep a lot when I was an anxious teenager. I used to render myself unconscious and be out for 48 hours at a time. So I did the same then.

I managed to re-negotiate the bank loan several times as well as extending the period of the car loan. Working it out on pieces of paper was fine. Keeping up with it was really difficult. John needed the heroin to be able to go to work so we were still spending £50 every couple of days, sometimes more. So it was at least £140 a week as a minimum for a little tiny bit that didn't do much for either of us but was better than nothing. Basically all that John earned went on heroin and that was before we bought food. My mother supplied us with loads of food from her freezer so that helped. It meant the difference between stealing and not stealing it. My whole family was extremely worried and tried to help. It was impossible to hide it. You could tell just by looking at us. Also one of us was always disappearing for hours on end.

I remember they offered us their house when they went on holiday and I sold all my father's sword collection and his silver coins and medals. I would do things like that periodically to reinstate my habit. Once while living at home I rang Barclaycard and got my mother's PIN number by pretending to be her. Obviously I knew the answers to all their questions. I discovered I could use the card to withdraw cash at dispensers. I used to catch her post and hide her bank statements for months. It felt dreadful. I couldn't understand how I could do that while at the same time I was doing it. I couldn't help myself. I couldn't stop myself. I had to shut off the awfulness of it all in the same way I shut off when my son drowned . . . the ability to just forget it otherwise I would just die of pain.

I knew I couldn't come off heroin even though I'd 'succeeded' in the past but that had only lasted for a couple of months and nothing else changed. It didn't make any difference whether we were on it or off it because inside and outside me it was still the same. But it was less so if I had my little security ball. So I relied on it totally and I couldn't give it up and so I couldn't stop doing these things, like stealing. So that's what I did. John hated it especially when I went to sell my parents' stuff. I had to do it so I wouldn't tell him. He never asked questions but he knew what I was doing. My mother found out and hid her cash card and my father stopped leaving money in his trousers pocket. They forgave me all the things I did – and didn't know half of them. I pawned some of my mother's jewellery, my brother redeemed it, I pawned it again and my mother hid it when she had redeemed it. And I couldn't find where she had hidden it which was a new one on me! I knew time was running out. I'd got the message that there was nothing I could do to stop myself using heroin. Also that it made no difference. But it was a cry for help to the people who loved me. I knew I couldn't go on like this. It was madness. Either I was going to die or I would be in prison or found under Waterloo Bridge. But something had to happen. I think I wanted someone else to take charge. It didn't matter who it was.

After my son Michael was born it brought it home to me how fruitless it all was and yet there seemed no way out of it. I stayed with my parents totally because I wasn't capable of looking after the baby and I didn't want him near me in case he picked all this up. I loved him so much I wanted to keep away from him in the state I was in. It was a safe place for us to be. By then I was drinking a bottle and a half of whisky or vodka, or anything, a day. I knew alcohol was a depressant but it helped to knock me out. But I also knew it might kill me. I didn't get help for myself in case my children were taken away from me and put into care. I was in an alcoholic blackout when I was awake and collecting methadone scripts again. John was working and taking methadone as well. The children were staying with my parents most of the time. I went to an agency for secretarial work but all they had was a job folding clothes in a laundry. So I took that. It was all I could manage to do. It was £2.80 an hour but we were desperate financially.

We had all the old debts including the car loan and a huge bank loan. John's monthly wages were gone in two weeks paying off debts. We had the bailiffs in at one stage for non-payment of fines and bills so I signed everything over to my mother so that I didn't own any goods or chattels. They kept sending letters which was awful. It was completely disempowering. I felt helpless because there was nothing I could do to stop them. This had been going on for a very long time. I suppose our debts totalled about £1,000 – apart from all the money I'd stolen from my mother. But it could've been a million pounds. It felt that huge. I kept it secret from my parents. Although they knew we were in debt they didn't know how much debt we were in.

The whole experience of being in debt with the bailiffs hovering felt like something we had no control over and no ability to get out of. It felt like a downward spiral that would get worse and worse. We couldn't rescue ourselves – we couldn't get out of it. Looking at it now I can't imagine why not! But at the time that's how it felt. It went along with not being able to break away from addiction which was running alongside all this debt. The addiction was going to go on for ever and therefore the debt would too. So it was like 'give up' time, the end... which was also the beginning but I didn't know that. I thought I was going to die and I was very surprised when I didn't. And even more surprised when I was eventually able to climb out of debt. It had been an ongoing nightmare. We had some laughs as well. The HP company thought we had a grey Lada instead of a brown Skoda so they drove past it hundreds of times. So we still had the car. We drove it without insurance or tax because we couldn't afford it. Eventually the company took us to court and the £800 became £1,200 with costs and so on and we are paying it off at £8 a month for ever. Now I sometimes pay £16 a month!

The turning point was when I went to a treatment centre that deals with addictions and stayed there. It was four years ago. I spent six weeks there learning to understand how it happened and that it was not my fault and that I couldn't have stopped it by myself anyway. This was a way of doing it. They helped to show me that all my behaviour – like stealing from my parents – was around needing the drug. I wouldn't dream of doing that now, but it related to being powerless over heroin. It was also about trusting in the universe – including this god or power that I didn't like – that was greater than oneself and that was not drugs. It was something else – the thing that made the trees green and the weather change... life goes on regardless and everything runs in patterns and cycles. I am part of that and being part of it I get that security back. This was what I was searching for in all those other things but it's within me and around me. So I'm not an alien after all! I explore that more and more – and little signs come in like 'my debts did not follow me' and they still haven't.

I don't know what's happened to them. I went into the treatment centre with a suitcase full of bills and county court judgments, including catalogue debts for clothing for the kids and money that other people had given me as an agent for the catalogue company. The staff at the centre said they were going to help sort me out, not the debts, and told me to put them in the basement. I was most disappointed. I was expecting this lawyer to come along and dissolve them all again like last time.

When I've asked for help honestly and truly without trying to hide part of myself, I've got it. I was never made to feel uncomfortable. I guess I still owe the debts but nothing has happened so I suppose they must've been written off. I suppose I've disappeared so many times it's been hard to trace me. And no single debt was very big. I remember signing my father's name as guarantor for something so they went to him for the money but after I wrote and told them the situation I didn't hear any more from them. My mother eventually discovered what I'd done with her Barclaycard which reached £4,000 but she wouldn't do anything about it because I might've ended up with a criminal record. She said she would rather pay it off and I could pay her back some time but I don't expect I will repay her. I've never paid her back. But one day I hope to – that would be fun!

Listening to other people's struggles with drugs and debts as well as learning how to manage in terms of practical living has helped me a lot. I saw myself as a very young child completely paralysed and hiding in a corner, not feeling that it was safe to come out and be. What I learnt is how to tell myself I am safe and the various ways in which to do that. I also learnt to be more comfortable with myself. I don't need to be terrified of anything any more. I also learnt how to deal head-on with a situation rather than avoiding it.

The best thing I did for myself and my family was to get help. Unfortunately this now costs money. It used to be that if you were on Income Support a proportion of the fees were paid by the DSS.

Personal addictions

But the government has changed the rules and this is no longer the case. It now comes out of the care in the community budget so it's more difficult to seek help from a treatment centre because any funding is managed by the local authority and you are competing with others for it.

It was the only thing that could've worked for me – being taken away completely from the situation I was in, having a lot of physical distance between myself and my problems and being in a very safe environment to slowly come out of it. After six weeks in the primary treatment centre I went on to a secondary care place where I stayed for six months. It was also good to be around people who were going through the same experience and to be helped by people who had done it already. It's reassuring to know you are not the only one. It's the same with debt. You need to seek help and to take the focus and the blame off yourself and turn the focus outwards to people who can help you and who are not going to judge you but will negotiate on your behalf. Also to talk to people who have recovered from debt. I think that a very large part of my recovery from debt was due to my changing my attitude towards it. Not internalising it so much. Trying to feel the abundance of everything and not worry about my own little bit. And of course not getting into further debt. Even millionaires are in debt – they just have a different kind of debt.

I would like to see an established network of women for women, particularly since we tend to worry about problems more than men and because it affects our relationship with our children. There should be places where we can go for help, advice and support, talk to each other and share our problems. This would help to change our attitudes and open us up to the possibility of positive change. I think as soon as people decide to make a change in this way they are open to all kinds of help – assistance comes from all over the place, like nobody has come back to me demanding I repay my debts. It happens. We need a more sensitive version of the masons, without the 'boys' own' capers, exclusively for women. It would be far more empowering than burning one's bra or wearing power suits and going to work as the manager. It's much more subtle.

For further details see Resources.

MARY: SHOPPING, SHOPPING AND BANKRUPTCY

Mary was a compulsive shopper. She loved buying and spending. It made her feel good and enhanced her self-esteem. At 29 she had twelve credit cards and debts totalling £20,000. It was easy to get credit, especially in the late 1980s, early 1990s. Finally she was forced to declare herself bankrupt.

Research in the UK on compulsive shoppers has recently been undertaken by Lancaster University. They are trying to ascertain how widespread the disorder is and why people become addicted. So far they have established that compulsive shopping seems to work very effectively as a short-term anti-depressant. It makes people feel better. It also gives them a kind of 'high', similar to the one experienced at the peak of physical achievement.

This disorder has been recognised in the USA since the 1980s where it is estimated that one person in fifteen is a compulsive shopper and that as many men as women suffer from it. Women buy clothes and jewellery and men buy golf clubs and electrical gadgets, but neither group has any real use for the things they buy. Pioneering treatment programmes as well as hundreds of self-help groups have been set up in the USA and cures include group and individual therapy, the ceremonial impounding of credit cards and debt counselling. Drug treatment in the form of anti-depressants is offered to the more severe cases. However, when the medication is gradually withdrawn the urge to shop returns.

Shopping and consumption are an ever bigger part of the way we live, and equating increased happiness with increased buying is becoming a way of life. The extent of the problem in the UK is unclear but there seems to be a need to set up self-help groups for people like Mary. Although she is in 'recovery', her fear – and the fears of those like her – is that without appropriate help she might return to her old patterns of behaviour.

I am 30. I started work in 1982 for a bank and it seemed to be a way of life to have store cards and credit cards. That was how it was. I was single and into having a good time like everyone else. I got my first credit card and I'd have a bit of a spend by going to London every month to see my friends and buy lots of clothes and things. I must've been about 20 when I got my first credit card. For the first three years or so I managed my credit cards all right, paying them off, going out and spending a bit but managing OK, until it got to the stage when I began paying the minimum back. Before I knew it I was applying for another card, spending it up to the limit and getting another card and spending money on that. I didn't think about the fact that they all had to be paid off. Instead I would think, 'I'll just do some overtime and I'll be able to pay it back' and gave myself a false sense of security.

I met this chap at around that time and moved in with him. It turned out to be a very hard relationship because he was a manic depressive and a body-builder to boot! He wanted me to be his perfect girlfriend and look good all the time. I think that was when it all started. I began spending to make myself feel better rather than just to have a good time. The money was not money – it was something to make me feel better about myself. He'd put me down all the time, so I'd go out on my own and have a shopping spree and that was a way of cheering myself up. At the time I felt very insecure and worthless so it was a way of helping me to lift my spirits, a safety valve, a kind of comfort. That was when things started getting bad.

I didn't buy anything in particular. I spent a lot on the house, making it nice. I also spent a lot on clothes and going out. I made lots of cash withdrawals from cash machines using my various credit cards and would go into Marks and Spencers and buy nice food – just nice things. I didn't have any obsessions like buying lots of shoes. I'd go into any shop I came to. My boyfriend didn't notice anything unusual. We managed our own money separately. I suppose he thought that all the things I bought came out of my wages. He was unemployed so perhaps he thought that I had so much more money than him and was able to afford anything. I supported him to some extent, although he'd do cash-in-hand jobs. I paid more than half the rent but that didn't matter to me at the time. It was just money.

At that time I had four credit cards and there was no way I could've managed to pay them all off. I could barely make the minimum repayments of about 12 per cent on each one. I kept up the repayments on the credit cards for about seven years but then it got to the stage when I could no longer afford to. I still spent money using my store cards. It was so easy to carry on getting credit, especially in stores. A shop assistant would say, 'Come on, just have a card.' That's what it was like a few years ago in the late 1980s. I remember when I was in a store and my friend was buying something. I was sitting outside the changing rooms waiting for her and an assistant came and sat next to me and said,

'Are you interested in a card?' I was not even buying anything! But I did get the card. I didn't want anything then but I thought it would be more money that I could have if I did want to buy some clothes.

Working in a bank meant that I knew all the right answers to the questions they asked on the application forms for cards. I knew which cards to say I had and which ones to avoid. Finance companies have a scoring system on each card. You get so many points per question and the more 'secure' you sound the more points you score. For example, if you have lived in the same place for three years, if you have a job and so on. I did not actually lie on the form, just a white lie here and there. So I was quite confident that I would always get a card.

Looking back I still didn't think it would be unmanageable. It didn't bother me at all until I got to the point where all my cards were exhausted. At that stage I owed about £7,000. I found an advertisement in *The Sun* newspaper for a quick loan and rang up. They gave me a loan over the phone. I got £2,000 straight away. It was the early 1990s. When I got the cheque I didn't pay off the cards because it was cash in my bank and I just spent it. Actually I went to three finance companies and got about £8,000 worth of loans. None of the companies knew that I was borrowing from the others at the same time. If the system was different – if they had a national computer to check on their potential borrowers – I wouldn't have been able to borrow like that. It was too easy.

The interest rates were extortionate – about 40 per cent – but I didn't think about that. I suppose I thought I would be able to pay it off. I had about £8,000 on my credit cards and a further £6,000 on the loans. I also had staff loans from my bank. You could get them at a very low rate of interest as long as it was for something in particular. I bought a new car. But I sold it after a couple of years and instead of repaying the loan I spent the money on a deposit to buy a house with another boyfriend. That loan was still outstanding, making my total debts around £20,000 including all the interest that had accrued. That was two years ago when I was 28.

Nobody knew I was in financial trouble. I didn't tell anyone. I think I wanted to and a friend remembered recently that I had hinted that I was in trouble. I vaguely remember trying to tell her but she didn't respond, so I left it. I think a few people may have wondered how I had so much money since I was on the same wage as them but no one ever asked. Outwardly I'm a very cheerful person and give the impression of not having problems. I'm good at hiding them. I don't know why I didn't tell anyone. Perhaps I didn't trust them or I was too scared to or I didn't want to admit it to myself. But I must've wanted to tell her because I obviously tried to.

I think I had about four or five years of torture, realising it was getting too much for me and thinking there was nothing I could do about it apart from borrowing some more – or until a miracle happened. By this time I wasn't paying anything off and I was receiving lots of letters. I used to read them and put them in the bin. After a while I just put them straight in the bin. I just swept it all under the carpet. It'd make me feel sick. I would think, 'Oh, my God, what do I do now?' And then I'd think, 'What's the worst thing they can do to me?' And I'd say to myself, 'I'll sort it out when it gets to a really bad point,' and throw the letters in the bin and just not think about it – or at least try to forget as much as I could; it was impossible to forget about it completely. That's how I handled it all the time – I just tried to forget about it.

It felt like it was very much my business and that was another reason why I didn't share it with my friends. I am getting better about that but that's how it was then. I was the sort of person that other people would share their problems with. I'd never tell them mine. I just used to cope with them on my own.

I've been having some counselling lately and looking back at my family I realise that no one ever used to talk about problems. The response to any major catastrophe was 'let's not talk about it'. Problems were never mentioned. When my parents split up I think my sister and I realised that they had problems but we never knew what they were or why he left. One day Dad and Mum split up. Mum said she didn't want to talk about it. I was 18 and had left home by then. That's how it always was. Even when we were growing up and in our adolescence, Mum wouldn't talk about anything. My younger sister had the same experience. We were never able to talk about anything. She's having problems now and is also having therapy. She's an alcoholic. She's like me – she can't talk to anyone either. She feels people will think she's stupid or is being over-dramatic. She's on Prozac. She's very creative and is a mature student studying art.

I don't know how much of my upbringing is due to cultural differences. My mother is Kenyan and my father is a Geordie. They met in Kenya when she was about 20. They married and we all came over to the UK when I was a young child. I don't know much about the way she was brought up. I think she's had a much better life as a result of marrying my father. But I have recently discovered that he had money problems as well. I wasn't aware of any money problems as a child but I don't have many memories of my childhood. It just seemed to be a whirl of moving around. We always seemed to be packing up and going places. I don't know why we kept moving – maybe it was because of my father's money problems. As a child I thought we moved because of my father's job but looking back I think we were running away from problems. Maybe I've reacted to my problems in the same way.

It was not until I met my husband that I was able to begin to face all the debts. I'd been looking for a miracle and perhaps he was it. I met him three years ago and he represented security. We got married quite quickly. He didn't know anything about my debts and I didn't tell him. I didn't tell anyone. It'd got to the point where I was too ashamed so that I dare not. Also I didn't know where to start. How would I explain it? I thought he might leave me. Also he had a really good job and a house and I thought he would look after me. I don't know if it was a conscious thought or not. But I felt safe. I thought maybe we could pay the debts off together, that maybe I could talk to him and he'd sort me out – save me. Looking back I obviously thought I'd wait until I was married before I told him and then I'd have some sort of security.

I was sacked from the bank shortly after I was married. I had been very scared at work because I'd been stealing money. It was a relief when they had finally found out. I'd been embezzling money – just small amounts – for about a year. My job had been as a business adviser and a personal banker. I'd see customers about various problems before they saw the manager. I'd been working in the bank for almost ten years. I suppose it would have been easy to steal money when I was a cashier but it never occurred to me then. I think when you work in a bank you don't see money as money. And perhaps at that point I didn't think I was in trouble. It was only when my debts amounted to more than £20,000, when all my wages were going on paying debts that I began to get worried. But I really resent the fact that no one noticed at work because the staff's accounts are usually closely monitored in banks. If that had been the case, my problems would have been picked up long before I reached the point of stealing money. When you're a bank employee you're not supposed to bank with anyone else or to have any other credit cards. I can't understand how they didn't know what was going on for all that time. They would look at employees' cheques from time to time. Obviously it's fair enough that they need to keep an eye on their staff. But in all that time no one picked up what was happening to me. They should've been able to tell that I had problems – like having an overdraft and money not being paid back. If they'd confronted me about my problems I think I'd have admitted them even though I was a bit intimidated by the boss. I might've asked for a big loan to pay them all off. That way someone would've had some control over it. I think I wanted someone to take over, especially in the last four or five years before I was sacked. At the time I mightn't have seen it as help – even though I needed it – and felt that they might've bullied me by demanding to know how come I had so many credit cards and so on. But I didn't feel brave enough to actually go up to someone and ask for help or to say I couldn't cope. But I think I would've accepted help because my job was at stake.

The branch I worked in was very small and possibly a bit lax on security. I had access to a dormant account that had thousands of pounds in it. I had opportunities to debit and credit it to my account because the security was so slack. Each time I did it I was very scared but because no one found out I kept doing it. I think it was another way of getting them to find out so I would have to come out in the open. I knew I'd get found out sooner or later because the auditors came round every six months and went through everything – so I must've known I was going to get caught. I stole small amounts to start with – about £100 to £200 each time and I did that about eight times so it amounted to about £2,000. It helped me a bit from month to month but it didn't help in the long run. I used it to pay off debtors who were writing letters threatening me with the bailiffs and it meant I could say that I was able to pay off, say, £20 a month. It was the only way I could keep them at bay. I suppose I could have asked my parents but that would've been very difficult because I can't talk to them about anything. Also I would've had to tell them everything and I couldn't. Perhaps I was scared of what they might say. I've never gone to them with a problem. Neither has my sister. They could have afforded to help me. At that time Dad had started earning about £100,000 a year.

I always had what I wanted as a child. We all did. My dad is a bit of a spender, similar traits to me. If my parents didn't have money they would buy things on their credit cards, so I thought that was normal. I never heard 'We can't afford it'. We always had everything that we wanted even when they weren't very well off. But I couldn't bring myself to ask them for help when I really needed it.

I got married and we went on our honeymoon for three weeks and that was shortly before I got the sack. I knew that the auditors were coming in and I knew they would find out while I was away. I can remember very clearly walking back into work and it was horrible. I felt sick. I knew that everyone knew what I'd done. They were looking at me in a funny way. I was hauled into a room and they said, 'This is what's been happening and you are in the frame.' I admitted it and was told to go home. I wasn't given a chance to explain anything at that point although I was eventually given an opportunity to do so. Then I had to walk all the way back through the branch with everyone looking at me. Actually the staff was quite sympathetic after a while. I suppose they didn't lose too much and I'm sure someone would have been in trouble for not noticing things earlier. I think that's why they decided not to prosecute me.

I'll never forget the day I got sacked. I walked to a park and sat down and cried for ages. I thought, 'I'm not going to go home. I'm going to run away.' My husband didn't know anything at this stage but I couldn't do that to him, so eventually I went home. A friend who was lodging with us asked me what was wrong. I said I didn't feel very well and went upstairs. He rang my husband who came home. I blurted it all out and he said, 'Don't worry, we'll sort it out.' He was quite calm about it. I couldn't believe it! He was great. He gave me a lot of emotional support all the way through it. He also gave me money each week because I couldn't claim benefit for 28 weeks as I was sacked.

I felt a certain amount of relief that it was all out in the open but I was really ashamed as well. I'd known all my work colleagues for over ten years and all my customers knew me. There are not many coloured bank clerks round here! It's a small town. I was known. I thought I'd never be able to walk the streets again. I didn't leave the house for ages. I couldn't go out for about six months. I used to sit in front of the breakfast telly in my nightie. Most of my friends dropped me, except a few, and even now they won't look me in the eye. It was a real shock. I've learnt a lot about people as a result. The only contact I had during that first six months was with my husband and his friends who were very supportive; and a few friends who didn't work in the bank. I still didn't talk about it during that time even though my friends were trying to encourage me to talk. My mum was weird. She didn't tell me off or anything. She simply said, 'Don't tell anyone else in the family.' And that was it! She still doesn't talk about it now.

I was concerned how she might respond to a TV programme that I took part in on compulsive shoppers. No one in my family knew about what had happened. I still don't know if they know. I did tell my two sisters. They wanted to know why I hadn't told them what was going on. They were shocked and didn't know I had any problems. I think part of the reason for participating in the TV programme was to let people know my side of the story, especially after the way some people had treated me. The whole experience of being part of that programme was very healing, particularly having the opportunity to talk about my problems with people who were not involved with me. Also the sympathetic way they responded to me. It was brilliant to know that people understood. The other aspect was the thought that I might be helping others before they got to the stage when their spending became a serious problem. It was very therapeutic. Talking about it really helped me to realise the importance of doing just that. It was like I finally admitted it to myself, although when I watched it, it did not seem like me!

The programme took place a long time after I'd been sacked. During that time it felt like there was no way forward. I was very depressed and had lost interest in everything. I remember thinking that at least I was married so I could be a housewife for the rest of my life and look after my husband, so I resigned myself to that idea. It felt like not just the end of my career – because obviously I'd never be able to work in a bank again – but also the end of my working life. I felt that I was going to be unfulfilled for ever which was horrible because I'm the sort of person who likes doing things and being independent. The worst thing was the shame. And all the people I'd let down. How could I have done that? I also kept wondering how I could've let things get so out of hand for so long. I couldn't come up with any answers.

Since I've had counselling I've realised that the whole experience was a lot to do with self-esteem. I know mine has always been low and I think that the spending had a lot to do with that: it helped to give me a boost. When I went shopping the shopkeepers would make me feel special. I was an important person. I had money. It was nice having a credit card in my hand. I suppose it gave me a sense of status, of power – that I was wealthy. The feeling didn't last for long because when I got home there was the cycle of feelings about knowing I couldn't afford it, then thinking 'never mind' and then going out and spending again. It was a cycle that was not achieving anything except to make things worse but it was also how life was for me. I got a kind of 'high' when I was shopping and I got that feeling as soon as I walked into a shop and thought, 'What can I buy?' I loved it. I felt I could have anything I wanted. I didn't need to shop around for bargains or to go without. I felt I could do anything I wanted. I could go to London, escape any relationship problems I had, take friends out to dinner. I did that loads of times. I am a generous sort of person anyway. I suppose doing that made me popular, made people like me. That gave me the power to get more friends. I didn't see it like that at the time – only looking back. I was 'Miss Popular'. I was the party girl, organising things, paying for things. It gave me a boost. I was quite popular when I was at school but not as much as when I was in my twenties and 'generous'. Also having money meant that I didn't have to stay at home because I was skint. I could do what everyone else was doing and have a good time. And that was very liberating. I never thought about what it might be like if I couldn't carry on spending. I thought I was always going to be able to.

That all came to an abrupt end when I was sacked. It felt like the end of the world. I was very down for months. One day when I was mooching around the house I saw a programme on TV about voluntary work so I got in touch with the Voluntary Association and worked for Debt Line for about a year which was brilliant! I must have decided that I wasn't going to sit at home after all. Something must have snapped. It was a gradual process.

Working on the Debt Line really helped me. I was advising people who rang in about what to do and where to go when they had got into debt. It was good to feel I was helping other people so that they didn't get into the same situation as me. There were only a few of us working there and they didn't know me or anything about my problems. I wasn't ready to tell them at that stage as it was only eight months after I'd been sacked. Working there was very healing for me and made me realise that I wasn't the only one who had money problems. It helped to take away a lot of the shame that I felt and helped to make me feel better about myself. I hadn't gone for any debt counselling myself and I didn't realise that there were such places available. I suppose I could've gone to a Citizens' Advice Bureau but I didn't think that anyone there would be able to help me. I felt very isolated and alone.

Working for Debt Line changed all that and I realised that there are lots of other people with similar problems. I worked there for nearly a year and got qualified as a Citizens' Advice Bureau adviser. I really enjoyed it and the next step was looking into counselling which led to my doing an access course which I have just finished. Now I have a place at university which I find hard to believe! I never, ever, thought I would go to university.

It was wonderful to begin feeling independent again. I had become very dependent on my husband after I'd been sacked, which he didn't mind at all. But I began to resent being a housewife during my six months at home. When I eventually re-emerged into the world I realised I wanted to be on my own again. He's a lovely bloke but he wanted a wife who'd play the traditional role of being at home all the time and taking care of him. He likes to support a woman which is what I wanted in the beginning. I'd messed up being able to take care of myself. But I also wanted my independence. He didn't mind at first but I suppose by that time his role for me was fulfilled. I've never admitted it before but although I loved him I think perhaps our marriage was very much tied up with my trying to resolve my problems around money. I still care a lot for him and we are still good friends. He was a wonderful support when I needed him. He didn't pay off my debts but he came to court with me when I was forced to declare myself bankrupt.

The court appearance was not as bad as I thought it was going to be. The judge asked me how I'd got into such a mess and I said that I'd been spending too much. He asked me if there was any way that I could repay the debts and I told him that I didn't have a job or any assets and that all the debts were mine and not my husband's. I was given the option of declaring myself bankrupt and I did. It was really that easy, much easier and not nearly as traumatic as I thought it was going to be. They were very understanding. I had to see an insolvency practitioner who was very helpful and got me through it. I felt immense relief after it was over. I was told not to ignore any letters from any of the finance companies and that they would deal with them all. They took over completely after that.

Looking back there are things I would've done differently if I'd known what to do. The first thing would've been to get help. If I'd known there was a Debt Line I'd definitely have rung them.

The service is confidential. It would also have been helpful to talk to someone who was not involved with me. I didn't get help until things were very much out of control. I would urge anyone who has any money worry, no matter how small the debt is – whether it's a vet's fee they can't pay or someone's business is going bust – to seek the appropriate help. I found that those offering advice for financial problems helped to take away the burden of it all. They can do this by getting all the details of the debts and, with the person's permission, write and negotiate. That helps to take off the pressure. Also they know the law very well, so if a finance company is threatening you with the bailiffs they can advise you that this isn't possible without a court order. They are a national organisation – part of the Citizens' Advice Bureaux – and get good results. People ring and say how relieved and thankful they are.

Another thing that helped me a lot was being part of a group. I found it helpful at the time to be in a group where I was labelled a 'compulsive shopper'. Your problem is the same as the others. I hadn't seen myself as a compulsive shopper. I read about it in a magazine. It described all the features of a compulsive shopper and I found myself putting a tick in every box! That was about three years ago. Although the label is a bit frightening it's also quite reassuring to know it is a problem. I think it's a psychological problem not an illness and it's important to have therapy or counselling of some sort because there are a lot of underlying reasons why people do it. For me it was about wanting to be liked, lack of self-esteem, the sense of power, the quick 'fix'. It was also about 'comforting' myself and needing that from others. I always wanted people to praise me. I wonder how much of it comes from not experiencing that as a child. Achievements were never acknowledged. I remember when I got my 'O'-levels I was thrilled because I got eight. My father simply said, 'Why weren't they all As?' Whatever I did was never good enough. So I was always trying to be or do the best of everything. My parents are still the same. When I told my mum recently that I was going to do a sociology degree she said, 'Why don't you do law?' At least I can recognise it now and not take it personally.

My other compulsion was food and over-eating which happened during this period as well. I ballooned from about 10 stone when I was 21 to 15 stone. My over-eating ran parallel with my overspending. I've lost 3 stone already this year because things are getting better for me and working out.

Personal addictions

It has taken two years to begin to feel OK about myself and to be able to walk around the town and go into my old bank. My mum used to try and get me to go in there with her but I always refused because I felt really scared. I still feel a bit uncomfortable talking to my ex-colleagues there and wondering what they're thinking. They're so over-polite. But it's not nearly as bad as it was. I've made new friends who don't regard what I did as being such a big deal. They like me for who I am. They have helped me enormously by being very supportive if I get depressed.

My sense of self-esteem has come through my achievements in my study and in getting to university. Everything is getting better and better. And it has got nothing to do with money! I feel even more liberated now because I haven't got money. I do things that don't cost money and it's so much easier because there is no stress attached to it. The difference now is that I get more pleasure shopping around for the cheapest bargain than knowing I can have what I want. I'm living on Income Support of £45 a week and managing quite well. I've got different friends now who are also on benefit so that makes it easier for me. I think the potential to over-spend is still there, but with counselling and in time I know I can cope. I know things are much better now. I don't have the same need to spend money, I don't feel materialistic any more and I don't feel deprived because of that. I'm happy just buying what I need to live.

It's been a slow process getting to know myself and feeling OK about myself. So much has happened as a result of all my problems. In a way I'm glad it's happened. My life has so much more meaning now. I can see my way forward.

For further details see: Chapter 16. Credit cards and credit agreements; and Chapter 17. Bankruptcy: three women's experiences.

Part Two

Managing Debt Positively

This section of the book is a practical guide. It offers information and advice to women wanting help with their debts. It is also designed to help women avoid getting into debt in the first place. It includes the most common reasons why women get into debt; information about women's rights; descriptions of the current law, benefits and procedures; names, addresses and information about organisations and agencies that offer money advice, as well as a list of useful publications.

The information on benefits and procedures is designed to be a helpful guide. It would be impossible to list all the different benefits and criteria for benefits in the space available. The information in this section was accurate at the time of writing but changes in guidelines, procedures and eligibility inevitably occur over time. This, together with the complexity of assessing eligibility for benefit, highlights the importance of seeking professional help as early as possible.

For this section I have relied mostly on a set of excellent handbooks published by Child Poverty Action Group (CPAG). The information in these books is accessible both to those in debt and to professionals in the field of welfare rights and money advice.

6 Women and debt

Common reasons why women get into debt

Many of the women I spoke to regretted the fact that they did not have enough information about their situation at the time they most needed it. They admit they did not seek help soon enough and many relied too heavily on the advice they received from 'professionals', such as a solicitor or building society manager, who in turn were themselves often inadequately informed or gave poor advice.

The key to managing debt successfully seems to lie in the measure of control the women felt they were able to exercise. This usually entailed a proper understanding of their situation: having as much information as possible about the facts of the case, their choices and the likely outcomes. The more control they felt they had over their situation, the more positive they felt about themselves and their debts. This in turn enabled them to cope more easily.

Getting into debt is most often due to unforeseen circumstances. For women this can be the loss of a job; loss of a partner; trying to live on a low income; borrowing because of a particular crisis or need; sickness; or having a baby. An unanticipated situation can trigger debt or make it worse.

How do you know when you are in debt? When does a loan become a debt? Whatever the cause of the debt, it becomes real when you discover that you are unable to pay back what you have borrowed. The next step is crucial. What are you going to do about it? What *can* you do?

Getting help

Financial advisers are trained to help deal with people's debts. They can help to negotiate a more realistic agreement about how and when (and sometimes if) these debts should be repaid. Some agencies (for example, the Citizens' Advice Bureau / CAB) offer a telephone helpline, emergency appointments where appropriate, as well as help and support. Agencies can be found in most towns and cities throughout the UK. (For details, contact the appropriate organisation's head office, listed at the end of this book under 'Useful organisations'.) Contact the appropriate agency nearest you or ring the local telephone money advice helpline. Your local CAB should be able to help you with this.

Regional differences exist in terms of help offered by local city councils. Some have their own money advice services. Special **telephone helplines** are made available to the public by some CABx such as the one in Bristol which also publishes a self-help guide for people dealing with debt. **Emergency appointments** are available for people who are faced with a crisis because of debt problems.

Bristol CAB's self-help manual gives the following examples of crises requiring emergency aid:

- a creditor is threatening to make you bankrupt and you do not want to be made bankrupt or you are not sure what it involves

- your gas, electricity or water is disconnected or about to be disconnected

- your mortgage lender or landlord has a court order against you and you are at risk of losing your home

Money advice agencies offer two clear messages:

1. **get help before a crisis occurs** in order to avoid more serious problems in the future
2. **it is not a good idea to borrow money to repay debts.** Nor is it wise to consolidate different debts by rolling them up into one loan, however attractive or cheap this appears to be in newspaper advertisements. It may simplify things at first but often makes the problem worse as you end up owing even more money. It is far better to be honest with those to whom you owe money and try to negotiate reduced payments.

Avoiding debt

Women are more likely to be vulnerable to debt in certain situations relating to their personal or professional lives. The following examples are drawn mostly from stories shared by the women in this book whose personal situations triggered a debt crisis.

- losing your partner (Laura, Alice)
- running your own business (Rebecca, Josephine)
- addiction to drugs, alcohol or shopping by self or partner (Mary, Emily, Margaret)
- using your house as collateral in business (Josephine)
- being a student (Isobel)
- divorce settlement and pension rights (Alice)
- house repossession (Jennifer)

Other circumstances include:

- losing your job
- having a baby – especially unplanned, or planned but not budgeted for
- sickness
- disability
- living on a low wage

Debt checklist

There are various types of debt and it is useful to identify which types affect you before attempting to deal with them. Money advisers will be familiar with all types. Generally they fall into two categories: credit-related debts and other payments owed.

Credit-related debts

These are dealt with under the Consumer Credit Act 1974. This legislation covers almost all aspects of personal credit and agreements. These include:

- bank overdraft

- bill of sale (securing loan by offering item of personal property)
- budget accounts (provided by shops up to agreed limit)
- credit cards
- hire purchase
- mail order
- personal loans

Other debts

Charge cards (for example, American Express) are included in this list. They differ from credit cards because no extended credit is given. The balance must be cleared in full by an agreed period, usually at the end of the month.

- charge cards
- business debts
- child support payments
- Council Tax
- fines
- gas and electricity charges
- Income Tax arrears
- maintenance payments
- mortgage repayments
- National Insurance contributions
- rent
- Social Fund repayments (outstanding loans made by Social Security)
- Value Added tax
- water charges

Is the debt valid?

It is important to have as much information about your financial situation as possible. The following may help you to establish some facts about your debts.

It is important to **ensure that the debts you have are properly identified as yours and that you are legally liable to pay them**. This point is highlighted in Josephine's story. She had assumed, until she saw a solicitor, that the business debt she and her partner had run up was a joint one and that as a result of this debt they would lose their house which they had put up as collateral at the time of the loan. However, this turned out not to be the case. Although their business failed, Josephine's solicitor was able to prove that the bank had failed in its duty to explain properly to them at the time of the loan the full implications of putting up their house as collateral. In other words, they had not fully understood what this agreement meant at the time it was made and on this basis it was not a valid agreement. It is now the lawful duty of the creditor to ensure that both parties are separately advised; also that the implications of the loan are fully explained and understood.

You must also **ensure that there is a valid contract between you, as the debtor, and the creditor**, or that there is **a legal obligation** on you to pay (for example, a court has ordered you to make payments).

Sometimes debts are valid but not yours if:

- the rules governing the ways in which money has been demanded are not lawful; for example, if you are being harassed – perhaps on your doorstep – by loan sharks or money lenders who charge exorbitant rates of interest on small loans. Three million people in the UK apparently owe money to loan sharks

- you have not signed any agreement

- as an agent for a mail-order firm, your customers have defaulted on payment (this will be the case only if you have invoiced customers separately)

- your signature has been forged

- the debtor has died but creditors are attempting to hold close relatives responsible. There are several possible exceptions here: for example, where someone had joint liability with the deceased, such as mortgage or Council Tax payments (as well as arrears on these). Seek legal advice

- the debtor was under 18 at the time the contract was made and therefore s/he is not legally responsible for it

- a contract was made under duress; for example, if threats – either subtle or physical – were used to persuade someone to clear arrears by taking out a further loan

- the contract was not entered into freely by both parties; for example, where someone has been persuaded by someone else on whom they relied for advice or guidance (such as the bank) to enter into a contract from which they did not benefit. This is not always the case, however, and recently a mother lost a fight for her home after a high court ruled that even though she may have been a victim of undue pressure, the guarantee she signed was still lawful. This undermines the outcome of previous cases, such as Josephine's, where wives or girlfriends have signed bank guarantees on their homes not fully understanding that they might actually lose their homes. The significant difference between these cases is that the guarantor in this latest case had been personally warned of the risk and advised appropriately

- you have been misled about the terms of the contract; for example, you were told that a secured loan would not put your house at risk

It is always important to request a full statement on any outstanding debt and check off your payments against it.

Sometimes debts are not accurate or may be reduced because:

- upon further investigation the calculations are wrong; for example, estimates on gas and electricity bills where the amount requested is higher than that consumed or where there are faulty meter readings or where no 'request for supply' of fuel has ever been signed (the *Fuel Rights Handbook* from the CPAG provides full details)

- you are entitled to a particular amount that should be offset against the debt; for example, where there are rent arrears but you as the tenant have had to spend money on repairs because the landlord has failed to do so

- the goods or services are faulty or unsatisfactory and you may be able to avoid paying all or part of the bill. This must be done within a reasonable time of receiving the goods or services and is often stated on receipts

- all creditors must be licensed. Ask for their consumer credit licence number if you suspect they do not have one; they might withdraw at this point. Your local trading standards department will usually know whether a particular creditor is licensed. In the meantime it may be advisable not to make any further payments

- the credit is extortionate. The court has the power to decide this and among the factors they may (but not always) consider are the age, health and experience of the debtor, financial pressures at the time the credit was taken out, interest rates at the time the credit was granted and so on. However, the court's interpretation of what is an 'extortionate' rate of interest – especially where the loan is very short-term – can be very high

You may have the right to be protected from harassment. This is where demands are made for payment that cause 'alarm, distress or humiliation because of their frequency, publicity or manner' according to the Administration of Justice Act 1970. Harassment is a criminal offence.

If you wish to follow up these points in greater detail, please consult Chapter 5 of the *Debt Advice Handbook* by Mike Wolfe of the CPAG.

7 How to get the most out of your income

If you are working and have financial problems it is sensible to seek specialist advice to ascertain whether you are receiving your maximum income.

This may include ensuring that:

- you are getting the maximum entitlements and rates of pay
- your tax liability is as low as possible and you are getting maximum tax relief; for example, the Additional Personal Allowance for children of unmarried couples or single parents, including widows and widowers
- you get all the appropriate state benefits to which you may be entitled

State benefits

These benefits (which apply to Great Britain but not to Northern Ireland) may be means-tested. You may be entitled to a combination of both means-tested and non-means-tested benefits.

Many people do not claim their entitlements because they are unaware that they are eligible to do so. As a result vast sums go unclaimed and those people are needlessly worse off than they might otherwise have been had they claimed their proper entitlements.

Means-tested benefits

You qualify for a means-tested benefit only if you have limited means or savings; that is, if your income and capital are sufficiently

How to get the most out of your income

low. You are therefore not automatically entitled to a particular benefit. Assessing your eligibility will involve a detailed investigation into your finances.

If you are working full-time you may be entitled to one or more of the following:

- Family Credit
- Disability Working Allowance
- Housing Benefit
- Council Tax Benefit

If you are working part-time, you may be entitled to any of the following:

- Income Support
- Social Fund Cold Weather Payments, Community Care Grants and Budgeting Loans
- free school meals

Working or not, you may be entitled to any of the following:

- Housing Benefit
- Council Tax Benefit
- Social Fund Maternity Payments, Funeral Payments and Crisis Loans
- education benefits (other than free school meals)
- housing renovation grants

If you are unemployed and looking for work you may be eligible for the Jobseeker's Allowance which recently replaced Unemployment Benefit and Income Support for the unemployed (see pp. 137–8).

Non-means-tested benefits

These benefits are paid as a right to those who satisfy certain basic conditions such as being available for work, disabled or widowed. They do not involve a detailed investigation of your finances. Your income and capital should not affect your entitlement. They include:

- benefit for people incapable of work
- maternity benefits
- retirement pensions
- child benefit

8 Losing your job

It is important to ensure that you are in receipt of the maximum benefits should you lose your job. You should also check existing benefits in case of any under-payment. The appropriate person to consult is a welfare rights worker or specialist in this field. Contact your local advice centre or CAB.

The following leaflets are essential: 'Unemployed? A Guide to Benefits to Help Ends Meet' and 'Jobseeker's Allowance – Helping You Back to Work'.

Redundancy

If you suspect you are going to lose your job, you should talk to your trade union representative, Citizens' Advice Bureau, Law Centre or a solicitor who specialises in employment law. You could also contact the **Employment Lawyers Association** (tel: 01895 256 972).

Make sure the payoff is correct. Check your entitlement to statutory redundancy pay. You will need to have been at your place of work for at least two years to qualify.

Check that your employer is acting within his or her rights, that this is a genuine redundancy and that he or she has followed proper procedures.

'Redundancy Handling' is a free booklet from ACAS the Advisory, Conciliation and Arbitration Service. Use it to check that everything has been done properly.

Jobseeker's Allowance (JSA)

This new allowance started in October 1996 and has replaced Unemployment Benefit and Income Support paid to unemployed people. It cuts non-means-tested state support from twelve to six months. It represents the biggest change to the dole system since 1948.

This new regime is much harder on claimants, who must:

- sign and keep to a Jobseeker's Agreement as a condition of getting benefit
- have paid sufficient National Insurance contributions to receive benefit which will be paid for the first six months only
- pass a means test after this six-month period in order to qualify for further payment based on your National Insurance contributions
- show that you are actively seeking work
- 'allow' the employment officer to 'direct' you as the claimant to undertake certain changes to improve your chances of getting a job; for example, to change behaviour or appearance
- lose two weeks' benefit if you refuse to comply without good cause unless you can demonstrate that a member of your household will suffer hardship as a result
- then apply for discretionary hardship payments

It is always worth claiming for Income Support. You might not be entitled to the Jobseeker's Allowance, or it might take time to come through.

If you have no money you should apply for a **Crisis Loan** from the Social Fund at your local Social Security Office.

- the maximum weekly benefit is £47.90 a week compared with Unemployment Benefit of £48.25
- if you are under 25 you will receive just £37.90 instead of £48.25
- if you are under 18 you will receive £28.85

JSA claimants who work part-time will be encouraged to return to full-time work with a **'back-to-work bonus'** of up to £1,000, payable when you return to full-time employment.

9 Mortgage payments and house repossession

If you are in debt and finding your mortgage payments difficult to manage, there are a number of issues you need to be aware of. Jennifer's story illustrates some of these issues and further advice is listed below.

Jennifer

Jennifer is 49. She separated from her husband a few years ago mainly because of his drinking and the huge debts he had run up, including mortgage arrears which he consistently refused to pay. He had always earned a good income as a financial consultant. After they separated, Jennifer and her two children lived on Income Support. She continued to allow him to borrow large sums of money using the marital home as collateral and as a result she and their two children lived under the threat of repossession for a total of six years. Finally their home was repossessed. He continues to earn large sums of money and she now lives in rented accommodation on Income Support.

Jennifer approached the building society about two years ago and asked if she could take on sole responsibility for the mortgage repayments, including the arrears, and to include them in an interest-only mortgage. But although the building society 'like to help people who want to sort things out', they procrastinated and a few days after her third visit to 'negotiate' further with the financial consultant she received a bailiff's letter for repossession in fourteen days. Jennifer thinks this was simply another example of their inefficiency and poor communication, not only with their clients but within the organisation. The building society wanted to keep her ex-husband's name on the deeds because they regarded him as jointly responsible for the debts, even though he was not paying them off. It was because he had defaulted on the payments that the family was evicted. The ultimate irony is that this whole sad situation could have been avoided if the endowment policy had been used to pay off the arrears instead of being cashed in by the ex-husband (it was in his name only) and spent. Jennifer attributes losing the house in part to:

- the gross inefficiency of the DSS. She often used to get several letters a day from them – sometimes as many as five – giving her conflicting information about the amount of benefit she was entitled to. She received different amounts every week although her circumstances never changed
- the gross inefficiency of the building society and their poor communication, not only with the other organisations involved but within the society itself
- the injustice of the building society's refusal to allow her to take on sole responsibility for the mortgage payments, thereby avoiding the trauma of repossession
- the poor communication between the various agencies involved, for example the DSS, the Trading Standards Office and the building society which cost her money
- misplaced faith in her (alcoholic) husband to keep up the mortgage payments and the arrears
- having no control over the money when they were married
- being given the wrong information from professionals such as solicitors; for example, being told that her husband's debts were automatically their joint debts
- also, her husband should never have been made responsible for the arrears because he was not living under the same roof and yet at the same time he was made responsible for the repayments as well

What would have helped?

- having access to more specialised help

- being put in touch with a solicitor who knew about entitlements and the DSS
- having independent advice regarding benefits instead of stumbling across the fact that she was eligible for Income Support and her children finding out at college that they were eligible for a grant
- knowing other claimants on Income Support who could give practical information on where to buy cheap goods and so on
- having some help or support during the six years she lived under the threat of repossession

What advice would she give to other women in a similar position?

- ensure you get **expert advice**
- keep yourself as **fully informed** as possible. This may involve ringing your solicitor regularly for up-to-date information
- after repossession **make sure you are not liable for any further costs**. In Jennifer's case the building society reckoned there was a shortfall between the sale of the house and the amount owing to them

Facts affecting families threatened with repossession

- About 1,000 families lose their homes every week in the UK. This 1996 figure is the highest level for four years
- it is estimated that 1.5 million households now have 'negative equity'; that is, their property is worth less than they paid for it

New hope for mortgage debtors

A more positive, humane approach to people having problems with arrears is being adopted and the need for more flexible and realistic repayment schemes is at last being recognised. In a recent landmark judgment in the Court of Appeal, the judges ruled that home owners could spread their arrears over the full term of the mortgage rather than the maximum of four years usually used as a rule of thumb in the county courts. This ruling offers hope for home owners facing repossession and takes account of people's changing circumstances – such as periods of unemployment, sickness and changes in the interest rate – without the fear of losing their homes.

Some building societies are also beginning to take account of people's changing circumstances and the anticipated difficulties that might subsequently arise over their inability to make repayments.

Home owners threatened with repossession may be allowed to stay in their homes until sold following another recent landmark court ruling (involving the Cheltenham and Gloucester building society). Most mortgage lenders insist on selling their repossessed houses as vacant properties, often at 15 to 20 per cent lower than their market value, a loss borrowers must bear.

The National Association of CABx said judges might now be persuaded to allow borrowers to stay in their homes while the lender conducts the sale, provided they agree to cooperate with the lender's plans, thus making 'the best of a bad lot' for those facing inevitable repossession.

Home owners on low incomes

At present only unemployed home owners on Income Support get help with mortgage interest payments, while those on low incomes get none. Shelter, the housing charity, is urging the government to adopt a new mortgage scheme to support home owners on low incomes, thereby reducing the number of repossessions. The scheme would take the form of an income-related housing allowance similar to Housing Benefit but covering mortgage interest payments. This scheme, which was proposed in November 1996, could be financed by reducing Miras (tax relief home owners receive on their mortgages) from 15 to 12 per cent. Of 800 home owners polled, four out of ten said they would be willing to help low-paid home owners in this way.

Some CABx and law centres offer free specialist legal advice.

What happens to your mortgage if you lose your job?

- **non-payment can lead to homelessness.** Contact your building society or bank immediately to notify them

- **get professional help** from a money adviser like a CAB worker to negotiate on your behalf. It may be that a helpful solution can be reached. For example, they can arrange for you to make interest-only payments for a fixed period

- **if you need more time, ask for it** rather than agreeing to a payment plan that is unrealistic. Be specific about the amount of time you require

- get an **agreement in writing** that the creditor will take no further action during this negotiating period. Do not assume (like Jennifer) that because you are negotiating with the building society you are safe

- get the same **help with any other priority debts** you may have, for example, gas or electricity

- **contact the DSS immediately** to see which benefits you may be able to claim

Mortgages and Income Support

If you are in receipt of Income Support you will find that initially it does not cover the whole mortgage interest. Many creditors, however, will accept half the interest until you are eligible for the full interest to be paid by the Benefits Agency. It will then be paid automatically to the creditor who will usually withdraw a summons for possession should there be one in force, or agree not to enforce a possession order should they already have one on condition that the direct payments are maintained.

Should you have mortgage arrears, the Benefits Agency will pay the interest plus the statutory maximum that can be deducted from your benefit towards the arrears (see below).

The rules governing Income Support in relation to mortgage repayments have changed due to plans to reduce public dependence on state benefits. They include the following:

- since October 1995 all home owners have to wait longer before claiming Income Support. **New borrowers** taking out a home loan will have to wait **nine months** after losing a job or falling sick before becoming entitled to Income Support. After that, half the mortgage interest will be paid for the next four months and thereafter all the mortgage interest will be paid

- for **existing borrowers** there will be no state help for the first two months; after that half the mortgage interest will be paid for the next four months and then all the mortgage interest will be paid

- Income Support will meet only the interest payments; you will still have to pay endowment premiums

- if you live with a spouse or partner who is earning you will not qualify for Income Support

- if you have savings of more than £8,000 you will not get Income Support

- if you have savings of between £3,000 and £8,000 you will get only limited help

- you will get state help only on the first £100,000 of your mortgage

The alternative is to pay for **private insurance**, but the choice of policies is limited. Many people, such as older or self-employed people, workers on short-term contracts or anyone with an existing illness, will find themselves ineligible (see Payment protection policies on mortgages, below).

Income Support claimants have a statutory right to have direct deductions made from their benefit to pay off priority arrears such as mortgage interest payments at a set weekly amount. There is an upper limit to the amount that may be deducted each week. You *have* to be claiming Income Support to be eligible for direct payments to be deducted and to benefit from the protection that this often affords the claimant – that is, that no further action will be taken by the creditor provided payments are kept up and that arrears are paid at a fairly low rate.

Ensure that you keep yourself informed about mortgage payments. Claimants on Income Support have lost their homes because the DSS has bungled direct payment of their mortgage interest.

Payment protection policies on mortgages

These usually pay the interest on your mortgage if you are unable to work through illness, accident or redundancy. You can take one out at the time of the loan or later. Some independent financial advisers urge caution, maintaining that these policies are very expensive and people are buying cover they often do not need. The accident and sickness element is often better covered by buying permanent health insurance. Also, these policies are short-term as they usually pay out for only one or two years if you have a valid claim. You could have another job long before that time.

These mortgage protection policies have been strongly criticised by consumer groups because so many people have discovered upon claiming that they were excluded from doing so.

10 Loans and grants

If you are a claimant and need to borrow money, the DSS offer three types of loan with various conditions attached to each:

- the loans are discretionary; if you apply for a loan there is no obligation on the DSS to offer you one
- any decision is based on the DSS's view (set out in national and local guidelines) of what level of priority your request warrants. For example, high priority is given to essential household items, bedclothes, etc. Always give reasons why your needs are high priority
- loans must be repaid as the agreement is legally binding
- the DSS decides how much you should borrow in the light of how much you are able to repay
- loans are nearly always recovered from direct deductions from your benefit
- you can make a direct payment at any time to pay off all or some of the debt

You may be eligible to apply for a **grant**. This is better as you do not have to repay it. You can ask for a grant and a loan at the same time and apply to have the loan converted to a grant should you be successful in getting one.

Always ask for a **review** if your request for any of the loans is turned down.

Budgeting Loans

You need to meet all the following criteria:

Loans and grants

- you need help to meet a one-off expense that you have not been able to budget for
- you have been in receipt of Income Support for at least 26 weeks before applying
- there is an upper limit to the capital you can have
- it cannot be for an 'excluded' item; for example, expenses in connection with housing repairs or arrears (there is a long list)
- the loan must be at least £30 and not more than £1,000 (less any other Social Fund loans you may have)

Crisis Loans

To receive a Crisis Loan you must satisfy certain rules which are legally binding.

The money must be used for an emergency, or it is needed as the consequence of a disaster, and it must be your only means of preventing serious risk to the health or safety of you or your family. For example, you have lost your giro and the replacement has been delayed; or you are waiting for your first benefit payment or wages and cannot get an advance; or it is needed for rent payable in advance to a landlord who is not the local authority if you are also awarded a Community Care Grant on leaving care.

You must be over 16.

There is a list of 'excluded' items as well as excluded people; for example, prisoners or those in full-time education who are not entitled to Income Support.

There is no legal minimum amount loaned but there is a legal maximum of £1,000 less any outstanding (Social Fund) loans you may have. If you have other loans you may get less than you ask for but provided you satisfy the basic rules you can ask for a review if you are not happy.

Repayments

There is no law dictating rates or times when repayments are made but loans are usually expected to be repaid within 78 weeks unless there are exceptional circumstances.

If you are unhappy about the rate of repayment you can make a complaint, but you must do this *before* you accept the offer of a loan. If any loan repayments are causing you hardship you can write to the Benefits Agency at any time, explaining why it is difficult for you to make repayments at that rate and asking for a lower rate over a longer period.

National Welfare Benefits Handbook from the CPAG contains further details on loans and grants.

11 Having a baby

Having a baby is not only very expensive – possibly the biggest expenditure a woman may have – but can have a serious impact on the mother's earning power and pension rights. In fact, having a baby can cost a woman as much as 57 per cent of her lifetime's earnings after the age of 25 – an average of £224,000 (according to City University economist Heather Joshi). This includes unpaid maternity leave, dependence on low-paid, part-time work during the child's early years and, consequently, minimal pension rights on retirement.

Eligibility for allowances

Statutory Maternity Pay

- you are entitled to **maternity leave** and **Statutory Maternity Pay** (SMP) if you have worked continuously for the same employer for at least six months by the end of the 15th week before the baby is due
- SMP is paid by your employer and lasts for 18 weeks
- you have the right to return to work at the end of this maternity leave period
- all women, regardless of how long they have worked for their employer, have a right to 14 weeks' maternity leave. At the end of this period they have the right to return to the same job
- those who have worked for their employers for more than two years have a right to a longer period of maternity leave. They are then entitled to return to the same job or similar up to 29 weeks after the birth

- the minimum Statutory Maternity Pay is 90 per cent of average weekly salary for six weeks, and £54.55 for the remaining 12 weeks

Contractual maternity pay

These schemes are much more generous than SMP. They have generally been negotiated by a trades union and should be included in an employee's statement of terms and working conditions.

Maternity Allowance

This is a National Insurance benefit and it has to be claimed from the Benefits Agency.

It is payable for 18 weeks at a standard rate. This is referred to as the 'maternity allowance period'. The earliest it can start is the beginning of the 11th week before the week in which the birth is expected, and the latest is the beginning of the week following the week in which the baby is born.

Women have to satisfy the insurance contribution conditions, i.e. that they have been employed for at least 26 weeks in the 66 weeks ending at the end of the 'qualifying week'. The 'qualifying week' is the same as for SMP but, unlike SMP, the period of 26 weeks need not be continuous and you do not have to have worked for the same employer for the whole of that period.

The rate at which you are paid – the higher rate of £54.55 or the lower rate of £44.50 – depends on whether or not you were employed during the 'qualifying week'. If you were, you qualify for the higher rate.

Maternity Allowance is non-taxable but is taken into account when calculating Income Support.

Once you are within the Maternity Allowance period in your pregnancy you can receive Income Support without having to be available for work.

There are strict time limits for all maternity payments and you need to claim at the right time.

Having a baby 151

How to claim

If you are working, SMP is paid through your employer. Some employers are not obliged to pay SMP. This may be because you are paid less than the minimum wage for SMP or you left work recently. If your employer does not consider you are entitled to SMP then he or she must give you **Form SMP1** with which you can claim Maternity Allowance. You will usually need to submit a certificate from your doctor or midwife giving the expected date of birth.

For further details see CPAG's *Rights Guide to Non-Means-Tested Benefits*.

Self-employed and unemployed women can claim Maternity Allowance of up to £47.35 per week depending on the amount of National Insurance contributions paid.

Women who are **employed** in the qualifying week (15 weeks before the birth) will receive the higher rate of £54.55 per week. This is payable for a maximum of 18 weeks.

If you are a member of an **occupational pension scheme** you should investigate the implications of taking maternity leave on your pension contributions. If you cannot continue contributing you should ensure that you make savings into some other tax-efficient scheme such as a personal equity plan (PEP) or a Tessa.

Maternity grants have been abolished but those in receipt of Income Support or Family Credit may be entitled to a £100 payment per child from the Social Fund (see CPAG's *National Welfare Benefits Handbook*).

Rights of pregnant working women

- if you do not qualify for either SMP or Maternity Allowance – perhaps because you have had a difficult pregnancy or are away from work for more than 18 weeks – you may be entitled to one of the **benefits relating to sickness or incapacity** (see Chapter 3 of CPAG's *Rights Guide to Non-Means-Tested Benefits*)

- if an employee is dismissed for a pregnancy-related reason she will have a claim for **unfair dismissal** regardless of her length of service. However, employees must have worked for the same firm for two years before bringing a claim for unfair dismissal to an industrial tribunal. Awards are fixed at a maximum

- pregnant employees who are **discriminated against** in areas such as promotion opportunities, pay or fringe benefits may submit a claim within three months of the discrimination to an industrial tribunal. Sex discrimination awards are unlimited

- the Maternity Alliance stresses that mothers returning to work after maternity leave are legally entitled to **return to the same job** or one of comparable status. Women workers have a right to submit a claim to the industrial tribunal

Legislation governing maternity rights is complex and additional recent legislation has been incorporated under the Trade Union Reform and Employment Rights Act. Your trade union representative or your employer's personnel department should be able to inform you of your rights. Your written contract of employment may contain details of your entitlement.

Disputes

If you are in dispute with your employer about the amount of or your entitlement to SMP you should ask for a written statement including the reason why SMP has been refused. If SMP is being paid, the statement should say for how many weeks your employer considers it should be paid, and the amount to be paid.

If you disagree with this then first consult your trade union representative to try to resolve the dispute through the **grievance procedure,** if there is one. You *must* act within six months from the first day which is in dispute or you will lose your right to have an adjudication officer make the decision.

If this fails, then ask the adjudication officer at your local Benefits Agency office to give you a ruling on the question.

CPAG's book, *Rights Guide to Non-Means-Tested Benefits* advises the following:

- take care to deal with the main points clearly and logically

- appeal to a Social Security appeals tribunal if you are not satisfied with the adjudication officer's decision (see CPAG's *Rights Guide to Non-Means-Tested Benefits*, p. 101)

For further information about maternity benefits send a stamped addressed envelope to the Maternity Alliance (address on p. 201).

A booklet, 'Maternity Rights', is available from Citizens' Advice Bureaux, libraries and jobcentres or from Cambertown, Unit 8, Commercial Road, Goldthorpe, Rotherham S63 9BL, TEL 01709 888 688.

Suspension of parents' payments

At last some product and/or service providers are recognising that women need **more flexible schemes** when it comes to repayments on regular savings schemes, endowments or a pension, particularly if they have had the expense of a new baby. Instead of imposing traditional penalties when repayments become difficult, some building societies are attempting to accommodate changes in the financial circumstances of new parents.

The following options may be available:

- **baby break pensions**. These allow policy holders to take a twelve-month or two six-month breaks from repayments in return for slightly higher premiums

- **revised mortgage repayments**. Where there are difficulties it may be that parents can extend the terms of the loan in order to reduce the size of monthly payments: for example, convert a repayment mortgage to an interest-only loan

- another lender enables mortgage borrowers on maternity leave to reduce monthly payments by half for nine months at any time during the loan, providing the loan has been running satisfactorily for a year and that it is worth less than 75 per cent of the property's value. For loans worth more than 75 per cent, the option is available after two years. Unpaid interest is rolled up and added to the loan at the end of the maternity period

- more flexible mortgages are now available that allow borrowers to overpay monthly mortgage payments when they are able to do so and to pay less when they are less well off

You should act as quickly as possible if you wish to switch loans, especially if you are already on maternity leave, as some lenders might be reluctant about taking the woman's income into consideration. Talk to your bank or building society manager.

Social services departments

Social services has a statutory duty to help prevent children from coming into care by offering help to families in desperate financial need. The stress of being in debt can affect other areas of people's lives so that they feel that they cannot be adequate parents.

Lisa was struggling financially and trying to cope both as a single parent and as a student. She was so desperate she went to social services asking for help with child-minding. She received nothing and within a year she was asking for her children to be taken into care as she felt she was not managing to care for them adequately. She still got no positive response.

If you have a child or children and are experiencing grave financial problems or a crisis that directly affects your child, social services departments are empowered to help either by giving direct financial assistance or assistance in kind (for example, food parcels) to parents, where such action can prevent a child from being taken into care. This power is contained in section 17 of the Children Act 1989. Although empowered to make these payments, in practice their response differs widely depending on a number of factors. In one part of the country, disconnection of a family's electricity or the threat of eviction might trigger some financial help to prevent a child from coming into care – particularly if the family is already known to social services – but elsewhere a grant may be arbitrarily withheld. One suggestion is to consider a challenge by way of judicial review. You will need legal advice (see CPAG's *Debt Advice Handbook*).

12 Separation and divorce

Separation

If you separate **permanently** you can claim Income Support as a single person immediately.

If you separate **temporarily** you will continue to be treated as a couple. Where questions of **'intention'** (for example, to stay together or to separate) are involved, you must be able to demonstrate an unconditional or unqualified intention to do so. It must not depend on some factor outside your control, such as whether or not you get a job (see CPAG's *National Welfare Benefits Handbook*, p. 291).

Rachel, a woman I interviewed whose story does not appear in this book, was refused financial help by the DSS when she approached them with her two young children after she and her husband had separated. Help was refused because the DSS believed that the couple had not really separated and that their intention was to continue to stay together. This assumption was based on a previous incident: the couple had separated once before but had eventually got back together. 'Suspicions' were confirmed when a Social Security officer rang Rachel's home to discover that her ex-husband was there. He was in fact visiting his children.

Several further, tearful visits to the DSS and attempts by Rachel to enlist the help of social services followed. Finally, her solicitor wrote a letter confirming the separation. After a home visit (at which I was present), the DSS decided that the couple did intend to separate permanently and Rachel was granted Income Support. However, the benefit was not backdated to when Rachel and her husband had separated, but only to the date on which he took up rented accommodation. Rachel could have appealed but chose not to do so because of the likelihood of further emotional trauma.

Reviews and appeals

If you are at all unhappy with a decision that you are living with someone when you are not, you should appeal or apply for a review (see CPAG's *National Welfare Benefits Handbook*, pp. 130, 153 and 261). You should consider carefully what evidence to put before the tribunal/review board in relation to each of the six questions they will most likely ask, which are listed as follows:

1. Do you live in the same household? If not, the cohabitation rule should not be applied.
2. Do you have a sexual relationship? Having one proves nothing, but if you are not, then it is best to say so. In practice you may not be asked.
3. What are your financial arrangements? If one partner is supported by the other or household expenses are shared, this may be treated as evidence of cohabitation. It depends on how these are shared.
4. Is your relationship stable? A stable relationship does not mean you are cohabiting (for example, living with a landlord).
5. Do you have children? If so and you live in the same household, then there is a strong presumption that you are cohabiting.
6. How do you appear in public? Officers may check the electoral roll and claims for National Insurance benefits to see if you present yourselves as a couple.

If your benefit as a single person is stopped because it is alleged that you are cohabiting, it is up to the Benefits Agency to prove that this is the case. If they do – and you are still entitled to benefits – then you should be paid as a couple.

When do you count as a couple by DSS rules?

Various rules apply when determining whether or not you still count as a couple by the Benefits Agency. The following examples are taken from CPAG's *National Welfare Benefits Handbook*.
You no longer count as a couple if:

- you are living apart and do not intend to resume living together

- you (or your partner) have been in hospital for 52 weeks or more
- you (or your partner) are a compulsory patient detained in hospital under the Mental Health Provisions
- you (or your partner) are detained in custody serving a sentence of 52 weeks or more
- you (or your partner) are staying permanently in local authority residential accommodation or residential care or nursing home

You count as a couple if:

- you both remain liable for Council Tax at your address
- you intend to resume living together, even though one of you is currently living away from the family
- you are likely to be separated for less than (approximately) 52 weeks.

Income Support
You will no longer count as a couple if the claimant is abroad and does not qualify for Income Support (there are exceptions). However, where your partner is abroad you continue to be treated as a couple and after four weeks the amount of Income Support you receive is that for a single claimant or single parent. You can get benefit without signing on if you have children under 16. Your partner's income and capital continue to be treated as yours for as long as the absence is held to be temporary.

Even though you may not be treated as a couple for the purposes of calculating Income Support, you may still be liable to maintain your partner.

You are still treated as a couple if you are temporarily living apart and the following applies: one of you is at home or in hospital, or in local authority residential accommodation, care or nursing home and the other is residing in a nursing home but not treated as a patient, or staying in a residential care home, or in a home for the rehabilitation of alcoholics or drug addicts, or in Polish resettlement accommodation, or on a government training course and has to live away from home (you have a right to housing costs for more than one home) or in a probation or bail hostel.

Claiming for children – who gets Child Benefit?

You do not have to be a parent to receive benefit for a child but you must be 'responsible' for a child who is living in your household. You can claim for any child under 16 or under 19 if they are in full-time 'relevant' education (that is, they attend school or college studying up to and including A-levels and the course lasts longer than twelve hours a week, not counting homework). Where benefit is concerned, a child is the responsibility of only one person in any one week. There is no provision that takes account of the child splitting his or her time equally between parents.

You are 'responsible' for a child if you are claiming Family Credit or Disability Working Allowance or Housing Benefit or Council Tax Benefit. You are also responsible when the child is usually living with you; that is, s/he spends more time with you than with anyone else.

Where it is unclear in whose household the child lives, or where s/he spends an equal amount of time with two parents in different homes, you will be treated as having responsibility if:

- you receive Child Benefit for that child
- no one gets Child Benefit but you have applied for it
- no one has applied for Child Benefit, or both of you have applied, but you appear to have the most responsibility

Income Support

For Income Support it is essential to look first at who gets Child Benefit and only where this is not decisive is it relevant to look at where the child 'usually' lives.

Where no one gets Child Benefit, you will be 'responsible' if you are the only one who has applied for it. In all other cases the person 'responsible' will be the person with whom the child usually lives.

Where a child for whom you are 'responsible' gets Child Benefit for another child (usually a teenage mother), you will also be responsible for that child (the teenage mother's child).

The *National Welfare Benefits Handbook* points out (p. 292) the importance of looking at who gets Child Benefit (when applying for Family Credit or Disability Working Allowance or Housing

Benefit or Council Tax Benefit) only where it is unclear whose household the child usually lives in.

Other living situations are also covered in this section where a parent may be applying for benefit, including those with children who are fostered, boarded out and living in residential care.

Additional Personal Allowance

This allowance is for children of single or unmarried parents to ensure that they have a tax allowance equal to that of married couples.

Divorce

Several women whose stories appear in the book lost partners through separation or divorce, including Alice and Laura. Their situations differ in terms of their ages and circumstances – Alice divorcing after 40 years of marriage; Laura with two young children separating from her husband – but each triggered profound and long-lasting financial difficulties for them.

Laura

Laura's husband bought what he wanted on credit: expensive clothes and shoes, skiing holidays with his mates, even a Porsche. Eventually he was declared bankrupt. After five years of marriage they split up, since when he has consistently refused to make maintenance payments for their two children to the Child Support Agency. Laura's solicitor is still pursuing the matter and is threatening to sue the CSA. Her ex-husband has recently moved from England to the Far East, which is outside English jurisprudence. The Child Support Agency has failed totally to retrieve any maintenance payments from him and, as a result, Laura and their two children continue to live on benefit of £75 a week while he earns around £60,000 per year.

Laura attributes this failure to secure any maintenance payments to the CSA's incompetence. The CSA cannot be contacted directly, so all communication is protracted.

Laura's ex-husband has failed to acknowledge overall responsibility for the maintenance of his children and regards his dealings with the CSA as a 'challenge'. Because the DSS provides a safety-net, he chooses to believe 'the state will pay'.

What would have helped?
Looking back, Laura wishes she had been stronger emotionally and had taken over the household accounts when they were together. She also wishes that she had accumulated some money in anticipation of their splitting up. She acknowledges that it would have been better to enlist help from both their families when she needed it, instead of perpetuating the situation by not admitting what was happening and covering up for her husband.

What advice would she give to other women in a similar position?

- maintain your independence and have your own (private) account built from up the housekeeping
- stick to your guns and cut up the credit cards with his knowledge
- take control of the finances and give your husband 'pocket money'

Alice

Alice's husband walked out on her after 40 years of marriage. She had spent most of their married life taking care of him and their two children. He did not permit her to work and expected her to do everything around the house. He retired on a good salary as a bank manager and cashed in their endowment policy and various other insurances and savings that Alice at the time knew nothing about. She is now living on a pittance, a few pounds short of qualifying for Income Support and all the other benefits she would have been entitled to. He is supposed to pay her maintenance of £10 a week but pays this only occasionally. Alice attributes this failure to secure a reasonable settlement in part to poor legal advice. She assumed that the local solicitor she saw was professionally qualified and had specialist knowledge in the field of divorce. She also assumed that he had her best interests at heart. Her assumptions turned out to be wrong. Her husband's apparent

Separation and divorce

hurry to secure a divorce was not only more expensive than a separation – which was what she wanted – but it left no room for any sort of negotiation. She was later advised by another solicitor that she could have insisted on a separation. If this had been the case, she may have had a right to a share in her ex-husband's pension under the recent change in law.

One in three marriages ends in divorce in the UK. And yet until a recent change in the law (July 1996), attitudes towards divorcing women meant that the courts were not always favourably disposed to their having a share, or any entitlement, in their ex-husbands' pensions. Since 1 July 1996 the Pensions Act has made it easier for divorcing couples to divide their pension assets between them and a wife has the right to 'earmark' a share in her husband's pension when he retires ('earmarking' is described in the introduction to Alice's story in Part One). Alice, unfortunately, was unable to benefit from this change in the law and as a result has suffered enormously in financial terms.

What would have helped?

- having an opportunity to resolve problems. Alice was not aware of the mediation service – although she would have had to pay for this as it is not legally aided
- having access to legal information or resources locally or perhaps to an advice centre for women or a woman-friendly-type advice centre
- having support around her both at the time her husband walked out and for as long as she needed it afterwards, particularly to help her deal with her feelings of rejection and injustice

What advice would she give to other women in a similar position?

- to get good advice you may need to **shop around for a good solicitor**, especially one offering legal aid (though their numbers are shrinking). Choose one who specialises in divorce. It may cost more than a newly-qualified solicitor would, but in Alice's experience it would have been worth it
- always **ask for details of likely costs and charges**. Ask to be billed at regular intervals, say quarterly or when the

fees reach a particular level. Alice continually worried about the likely cost of legal fees but was never at any stage informed of the amount. Nor did she ask. She has been left with a huge solicitor's bill and no means of paying it

- **do not rush into divorce**, especially if you are unsure about it. Ensure that you have exhausted all the alternatives such as marriage guidance, counselling, the church. Once you start proceedings they assume a momentum of their own

- **consider mediation:** it is voluntary and you can decide what issues you wish to discuss and how you wish to resolve them. It could mean a satisfactory solution and settlement, with the result that everyone benefits. One of Alice's biggest regrets was that she was not given an opportunity to secure a more amicable end to their long relationship. Nor did she have an opportunity to discuss finances directly with her ex-husband. Instead she was left with a feeling of devastation and rejection, exacerbated by the shock and suddenness of his leaving and with no means of redress

- **resolve as much as you can yourselves**. Alice wanted to have the opportunity to do this at the outset but was unaware that she could simply get good practical advice from a solicitor and then try and resolve things with her husband. She did not realise that you do not necessarily need to rely on a solicitor to sort out problems

- **make sure you understand exactly what is going on** in the communication between the solicitors, especially regarding any agreements proposed or reached. Alice discovered several bits of important information from her new solicitor but only after the divorce: she discovered that the maintenance her ex-husband was paying was index-linked, and that a 'clean-break settlement' is agreed once the house is sold. Having this information at the time would have helped to reduce her anxiety

Pensions

The law on the issue of divorcing wives having a right to a share in their husbands' pensions has now changed. From July 1996 courts have been obliged to take pensions into account, either by balancing the value of other assets at the time of divorce, or 'earmarking' the (usually) husband's pension on divorce. Pensions are now often regarded as a couple's greatest asset, potentially being worth more than their homes. In Alice's case it was completely overlooked. She would otherwise have stood to gain considerably more than she has ended up with. At the very least she would have had a right to a 50 per cent share in her husband's occupational pension. It may be that she now has grounds for a negligence action against her former solicitor but this would incur further costs that she is unable to afford, even with some financial help from legal aid.

Be clear about what you want

Often in divorce proceedings there are unresolved issues between couples. These may include money: how it was spent, who spent it, who managed it, the rows it may have caused. For women in particular they may also include feelings about self-worth. Many women have no control over the family finances during their marriage and have never earned any money in their own right. They have no separate bank account or their own chequebooks. They are dependent on their husbands for money for housekeeping, clothes and so on, and for paying all the bills. If they do earn any money they put the family's needs first. They often go without things in order to economise; they budget. The issue of their own worth may therefore be an unfamiliar one and needs to be addressed thoughtfully by both the divorcing woman and her adviser.

Alice was married for 40 years and now lives on very little. She has no entitlement to her ex-husband's substantial savings that he accrued as a bank employee (he became a bank manager) – while she took care of him and his children at home – or to his very generous pension. Women of Alice's generation usually overlooked their own career needs to take care of their husbands and children. It is these same wives – who enabled their husbands to climb the career ladder and earn increasingly bigger salaries – who are often left bereft, their contribution ignored. To some, like Alice, it feels as if their lives have, in effect, been negated.

Taking care of husbands and children is often very undervalued and is sometimes recognised only after it is too late – hence bitter comments like Alice's that, looking back on her 40 years of marriage, she felt like an unpaid housekeeper.

Be prepared to bargain

You are most probably going to have to compromise. If you have no children it may be best to go for a **clean-break settlement** where the assets are shared and that is the end of any financial contact. Unfortunately for wives like Alice, this settlement is not cut and dried. Her clean-break settlement is dependent on the sale of the house which has been on the market for about two years, and that is something which is beyond her control. In the meantime she is unable to pay off any of her debts.

If there are children, the main breadwinner will almost certainly need to pay **maintenance**, see below.

The importance of achieving a positive outcome

Divorce is usually a difficult time for everyone involved, including the children. Money and property can be the source of acrimony which can permeate lives long after divorce. Two women in particular (Alice and Laura) still feel bitter and angry at the outcome of the financial 'arrangements' of their marriages and at the injustice of it all. They have both wondered how it could have been different or better. Laura is aware that the anger she feels at her ex-husband influences her attitude towards him in her dealings with their children but finds it difficult to change this at the moment. Alice is attempting to survive an impoverished and embittered old age alone.

One way of avoiding disputes and bitter disagreements that arise when divorcing couples have to divide up their possessions is to draw up a **marriage contract** before the wedding. Although they are not legally binding, in practice there is no reason not to honour the couple's wishes. Contracts vary depending on the couple's circumstances: for example, they might stipulate that all property owned before the marriage remains separate and that everything acquired during the marriage is split equally.

Solicitors recommend **reviewing contracts** at important times like the birth of a child. This would avoid the following common situation: when property is split equally between two partners, one partner – usually the mother – is faced with looking after the children without any additional financial help from the other.

Maintenance of children and the Child Support Agency (CSA)

If you separate from the father of your child/ren and want a legally enforceable child maintenance agreement you have to use the CSA. Liability cannot be put into effect until after an application is made. This applies whether or not you are a benefit claimant.

If you have care of a child and make a claim for Family Credit or Disability Working Allowance and you have not already applied for child maintenance, you will be contacted by the CSA.

Useful information about the CSA

The CSA was created by the Child Support Act 1991 and came into force in April 1993 to:

- assess and enforce the payment of child maintenance
- require those parents claiming certain benefits and caring for children not living with their other parent to apply for child maintenance or face a reduction in benefit
- arrange for collection of payments where requested
- decide about collection and enforcement of payments on behalf of the Secretary of State. Many of these decisions are discretionary so there is scope for negotiation with the CSA staff. The welfare of any child likely to be affected must be taken into account: for example, possible risk of harm or undue distress to the child should there be direct contact with the absent parent

Some decisions – like the assessment of how much the absent parent should pay – cannot be altered except by review or appeal. The underlying principle is that *both* parents have a duty to contribute to the maintenance of their child.

The courts are no longer involved in setting child maintenance (with a few exceptions).

If you are a parent with care of the child/ren and not claiming Income Support, Family Credit or Disability Working Allowance, you cannot apply to the CSA if you already have a court order for maintenance or a pre-April 1993 written agreement. Benefit claimants in the same circumstances, however, are required to apply to the CSA. The subsequent assessment may override any court orders they may have for child maintenance.

Benefit claimants are also under a 'special' obligation to authorise the CSA to take action to recover maintenance and to cooperate with the CSA to provide the necessary information needed to pursue the absent parent. The CSA cannot do this without your authorisation as the parent with care.

Unless you can convince a child support officer that you have good cause for withholding permission – for example, risk of harm or undue distress to you or your children – you will be penalised and suffer a reduction in benefit.

CPAG advises people not to give authorisation until just after the issuing of the benefit penalty in order to obtain a right of appeal (see CPAG's *Child Support Handbook*, p. 101).

Parent with care on Income Support

- you have 'special' requirements or obligations to **cooperate with the CSA** (see above) or else be penalised by reduction in benefit
- **payments** of child maintenance may be made either direct to the person with care or via the CSA which arranges to collect maintenance payments
- absent parents with a **poor payment record** may have to pay direct to the CSA
- **all payments are treated as income** and are converted into a weekly amount, if paid regularly, for Income Support calculation; for example, where payments are made monthly multiply by 12 and divide by 52. Where payments are not regular, each payment is divided over the weeks since the last payment
- this also applies where payments are made to the child

Separation and divorce

- **Income Support will be reduced** according to the amount of income you receive in the form of child maintenance payments

- lump sums are also treated as income not capital

- **make sure your benefit is not reduced until maintenance payments are actually made.** Reductions are sometimes made when the CSA sends notification of assessment but arranging payments can take time

- where payments are made via the CSA, you will receive one order book or giro cheque from the Benefits Agency which includes both Income Support and child maintenance. Your order book is cashable whether or not the absent parent pays but what you receive represents only Income Support. While the advantage is that you avoid direct contact and any disagreements that may arise, the disadvantage is that you do not know automatically if maintenance payments are being made. However, you can request a payment statement (make it in writing)

- from April 1997 parents with care who are not lifted off Income Support by receipt of child maintenance will build up a **maintenance bonus** of £5 a week. This bonus will be paid as a lump sum if you leave Income Support to take up work of 16 hours or more a week

Coming off benefit
This may happen as a result of having an income from child maintenance that is too high to qualify for Income Support. This means you are dependent on the CSA to collect the payments. If this fails you will need to make a fresh claim for Income Support. If there is any delay, contact the CPAG which is lobbying for better procedures.

The CSA has the power to decide:

- the amounts and method of payments by the absent parent

- how it should be collected. This could involve the use of its **collection service**, which means that there is no contact between you and your child's father. You receive the payments irrespective of whether or not the absent parent has paid

- whether or not to let you use the collection service (if not, contact the CPAG)
- the timing of payments
- the amounts of payments towards arrears

This may happen whether or not you are a claimant. However, if you were not claiming at the time of your application for child maintenance, the CSA can arrange payment only if it is requested by you as the applicant. The CSA can refuse. (If it does refuse, contact the CPAG.)

What happens when the absent parent defaults on payment?

Although the Child Support Agency was set up to ensure that both parents have a duty to contribute to the maintenance of their child/ren and it has the power legally to enforce this, the reality is that this does not always happen – despite the procedures that the CSA is obliged to follow.

The latest figures (published in November 1996) show that barely one in five absent fathers traced by the Child Support Agency is paying the full maintenance ordered. Only 21 per cent were paying in full in August 1996, down from 25 per cent in May. The proportion of traced fathers paying nothing has stayed stable at 41 per cent, with the remaining 31 per cent paying up in part. Laura's ex-husband is one of the 41 per cent of fathers who have been traced and who pay nothing.

There are various procedures that the CSA can set in motion to attempt to retrieve maintenance payments. These include the following: **enforcement** of payment which can be made in a number of ways through: (1) a **deduction from earnings order** which can be made by CSA staff; or (2) a **liability order** in the magistrates court if (1) above cannot be implemented and arrears exceed £25 and there is no arrears agreement or it has been broken. If this is granted, the Agency can **seize goods** using bailiffs.

Thereafter the court can issue a **distress warrant** – often almost automatic – which can be used if the debtor fails to pay

Separation and divorce

an amount ordered by the court, or one of two other orders: a **charging order** (where there is a charge placed on property owned by the liable parent so that should the property be sold the amount that is liable goes to the CSA); or a **garnishee order** which names a person who owes the liable person money (for example, a particular creditor) and requires that person to release funds up to the value stated on the liability order to the CSA.

If this fails, the CSA can apply to the magistrates court to commit a person to **prison** (the maximum is for six weeks). It is unlikely that the CSA would continue to pursue the arrears after a period of imprisonment.

Laura's husband has not experienced any of these procedures, as far as she knows.

Client dissatisfaction with the CSA

Laura believes that her husband's failure to pay is partly to do with the way in which the CSA is run. In fact, the vast majority of complaints about the CSA are about poor administration; in April 1995 50 per cent of uncleared cases were over a year old. The CSA admits it has failed to administer the scheme properly. The other major area of complaint from users is lack of flexibility in difficult cases.

Laura has contacted her MP, and her solicitor, as already stated, is currently threatening to sue the CSA. Her case highlights how much more complex the issue of maintenance – and the legal means necessary to pursue it – has become. Prior to the existence of the CSA, access to legal advice in divorce and maintenance cases used to be comparatively straightforward and legal aid was more widely available to people. Now it is recommended by the CPAG and other organisations that you need expert advice to be represented. In Laura's case, even this is inadequate.

CPAG's *Child Support Handbook* states that most CSA clients have remained on Income Support; they have not gained and many are worse off.

13 Single parents: maximising income

Since April 1997, benefits for lone parents – the £6.30 a week **One Parent Benefit** and the £5.20 a week **Lone Parent Premium**, both of which were frozen in 1996 – have been scrapped and incorporated into other statutory allowances.

Single parents who work more than sixteen hours a week and need to pay a child-minder can disregard up to the first £40 child-minding costs in calculating income for Family Credit, Housing Benefit, Council Tax Benefit and Disability Working Allowance. This does not apply to Income Support. The child-minder must be registered with the local authority.

Claiming One Parent Benefit might mean that your income for the purposes of Income Support is too high. As a result you might be taken off Income Support so you should calculate if it is worth it. If you are not on Income Support you will not qualify for free school meals or access to the Social Fund (DSS loan). If you are not sure how to do the 'better off' calculation get advice.

If you claim Income Support within three months of the birth of a child, claim a **maternity payment** from the Social Fund. The maternity expenses payment is £100 for each child. If this is inadequate you could apply to the discretionary Social Fund for the extra amount you need. CPAG's *National Welfare Benefits Handbook* says that although discretionary payments cannot be made for any maternity expenses, this is open to challenge. (For further details see CPAG's *National Welfare Benefits Handbook*, pp. 103, 372–3.)

You can claim extra tax relief through the **Additional Personal Allowance** whether you are a single parent or an unmarried couple with children (see below).

You are not required to sign on as available for work while you are claiming for a child under 16. Nor can any voluntary

Single parents: maximising income

unemployment deduction be made if you lose a job, for example through misconduct.

Maternity expenses

You are entitled to help with maternity expenses if:

- you or your partner are on Income Support, Family Credit or Disability Working Allowance *and*
- you do not have too much capital (the amount reduces if you have over £500) *and*
- you or a member of your family are expecting a child within the next eleven weeks or have recently given birth or have adopted a child *and*
- you claim within the time limits: any time from the 11th week before your expected week of confinement (your 29th week of pregnancy) until three months after your actual date of confinement

If you adopt a baby, you can claim up to three months following the date of the adoption order.

If you claim late you will be paid only if you show good cause for not claiming in time. However, you cannot be paid if you claim more than twelve months after the date of confinement or adoption.

How to claim

Use form SF100 obtainable from your local Benefits Agency.

The date of claim is the date the form is received by the Benefits Agency.

If you claim before your confinement you will need to submit a maternity certificate (form MAT B1) or note from your doctor or midwife.

Maintenance payments

You are entitled to maintenance payments for your children whether or not you were married and possibly for yourself if you were married. You are required to apply for child maintenance (see CSA, above) if you claim Income Support or Family Credit or Disability Working Allowance unless you are exempt and the money you get affects your benefit (see CPAG's *National Welfare Benefits Handbook*, p. 114).

Additional Personal Allowance

This allowance is for the children of single or unmarried parents to ensure that these parents have a tax allowance equal to that of married couples. As it is, some unmarried couples who live together may be paying too much tax.

This is an allowance that often goes unclaimed. One theory is that the title of the Inland Revenue leaflet IR92 ('A Guide for One Parent Families') is misleading because it does not make clear that *unmarried* couples with a child can also claim this allowance, even when living as a two-parent family. (Someone complained that the original title on the leaflet deters such people from reading it and the Revenue has agreed to change it to include a sub-heading: 'including unmarried couples with a child'.)

Eligibility

You can claim this allowance if:

- you cannot claim the Married Couple's Allowance: this includes widows and widowers, single parents and unmarried parents
- you are a man whose wife is totally incapacitated – but not if you are a woman whose husband is incapacitated!
- the child – who does not have to be your natural child – is under 16 or in full-time education
- you are an unmarried couple living together with children from previous relationships. However, you can claim only *one* allowance, regardless of the number of children you are bringing up
- you claim only for the youngest qualifying child in the household

Single parents: maximising income

- you are a separated couple with two children who divide their time between you. This entitles *each* of you to claim a full allowance in the year that you separate. The one who keeps the child/ren can claim the Additional Personal Allowance for the full year but the amount will be cut by any Married Couple's Allowance received. A husband claims all the Married Couple's Allowance! So if his wife has care of the child after they separate she can claim the Additional Personal Allowance for the full year as well

- you are a lesbian or gay couple and can each receive the allowance provided you have at least one child each

A **widow** claiming the widow's bereavement allowance can also claim the Additional Personal Allowance in the second year, when she is not entitled to the Married Couple's Allowance.

The allowance is £1,790 but tax relief is allowed at only 15 per cent, the same as the Married Couple's Allowance. Your tax bill is reduced by £268.50 a year.

You can backdate an application for unclaimed relief for the past six years.

Mike Wolfe in the *Debt Advice Handbook* suggests it is important to check on your position – particularly where a single parent who has been on Income Support begins to live with someone who is working. You can check your entitlement by looking at the tax code of the person who is working. The tax code is the person's allowance divided by ten. If Additional Personal Allowance is payable, the amount should be the same as that of a person getting the Married Couple's Allowance.

This allowance should always be transferred to the working partner immediately.

For further details of other tax allowances, see the *Daily Mail Tax Guide*.

14 Benefits for parents on low pay

You may be eligible for any of the following benefits provided you meet the criteria:

- Family Credit
- Disability Living Allowance
- Housing Benefit
- Council Tax Benefit

Family Credit

This is a tax-free benefit for low-paid workers with children.

You can claim it for six months. To qualify you must: work **16 hours or more a week**. If your hours fluctuate, then an average of 16 hours a week, *and* you are employed at the date of your claim, *and* you are paid for your job or (genuinely) expect to be paid.

Work can include self-employment, including people who work from home such as child-minders, carers and writers. The work must be your usual work and you must be likely to continue in that job for at least five weeks after you make your claim.

You or your partner must be responsible for at least one child who is a member of your household. You do not have to be their natural parent.

You are considered as not being in work and therefore cannot claim Family Credit if:

- you are on a course of education as a student
- you are on a scheme for which a training allowance is paid

- you are working for a charitable or voluntary organisation where only your expenses are paid
- you are a carer paid by the health or local authority or a voluntary organisation for looking after someone who is not normally a member of your household

If your claim is refused, claim again in the first week in which you work 16 hours or more. It may be that the claim has been held up by the Benefits Agency.

Make sure that you ask for your new claim to be **backdated** to the first week in which you actually worked 16 hours or more.

Ensure that you calculate all the hours you actually worked and were paid for. You can also include any hours you worked extra but for which you were not paid.

It may be that you fail to qualify for either Income Support (because you work full-time) or for Family Credit (because the work is held to be not the work you normally do). You may also be refused both Income Support and Family Credit because the adjudication officers at the Benefits Agency and at the Family Credit unit have a difference of opinion in interpreting the rules on the same facts. If this is the case, the *National Welfare Benefits Handbook* suggests you appeal against both decisions and ask for them to be heard together so a tribunal can decide which benefit is appropriate.

In the meantime, the *Handbook* suggests you could apply for interim payments but stresses that you will be eligible for an interim payment only if you are appealing and it is clear that you are entitled to some benefit.

Family Credit and Disability Working Allowance

You cannot get Family Credit if you or your partner receives Disability Working Allowance. This does not apply if your Disability Working Allowance is due to expire within six weeks of the date you claim Family Credit, *and* you fulfil all the other conditions to entitlement to Family Credit, *and* you are claiming for Family Credit for the period immediately after your Disability Working Allowance ends.

In all other cases you have to wait until your Disability Working Allowance award comes to an end before claiming Family Credit (see CPAG's *National Welfare Benefits Handbook*, pp. 134, 172, 176).

Check whether you are better off claiming Family Credit or Disability Working Allowance.

Disability Working Allowance is usually paid at a high rate and entitles you to a disability premium for Housing Benefit and Council Tax Benefit.

Disability Working Allowance

This is a tax-free benefit for low-paid workers with a disability – either physical or mental – which puts you at a disadvantage in getting a job. It is a weekly payment which usually continues at the same rate for 26 weeks regardless of changes in your circumstances.

Eligibility

You can claim this allowance if

- you are aged 16 or over
- your income is low enough
- your savings and capital are not worth more than £16,000
- you live in Great Britain
- you usually work full-time – that is, more than 16 hours a week
- you have a physical or mental disability which puts you at a disadvantage in getting a job
- you are or have recently been getting a sickness or disability benefit (see CPAG's *National Welfare Benefits Handbook*, p. 194, for a list)
- neither you nor your partner is getting Family Credit instead

To claim you simply have to sign a declaration that you have a physical or mental disability which puts you at a disadvantage in getting a job. This will be accepted unless there is some other evidence to indicate that you do not fulfil the requirements.

15 Business debts

The 1980s was the decade of instant credit and booming business. Money was easy to borrow and banks were keen to lend it. Increasing home ownership meant that more and more people like Rebecca and Josephine and their partners were easily able to borrow large sums of money to set up or to expand their businesses against the increasing value of their homes.

Both their businesses failed. Both couples had used their homes as guarantees against their businesses failing. Both women deeply regret doing this and stress that there are ways other than using your home to guarantee against the failure of your business, or your partner's business.

Rebecca

Rebecca started up a clothing design business in children's clothes in the mid-1980s. She soon realised that it was 'almost impossible to make money on a small scale' and set about borrowing the money she needed from her bank in order to expand. Although her business was successful initially and she was employing about 40 people at one time, it ultimately failed with disastrous consequences for her and her family.

Rebecca attributes the business failure to greed on the part of the investors whom she felt were concerned only with making a quick profit, and naïveté and a total lack of business experience on her part.

What would have helped?

- genuine, appropriate, **constructive help from the enterprise agencies**, especially in the early stages. This should have involved working together on common goals rather than the agencies dictating what they saw as her needs

- a **basic training in business** as a condition of any business loan
- the **banks should recognise the huge responsibility they have in lending money** and respond accordingly. If you borrow money from a bank in Germany, Rebecca says, not only are you asked to produce a business plan as in the UK, but often the bank appoints someone to see your business in operation (perhaps attending a board meeting), so that not only will the bank employee know about your business but s/he will also be gaining valuable experience in the world of business
- **a more positive view of women in business**. The assumption is that women do not understand finance and that is quite a powerful legacy, says Rebecca
- **people should be taught in schools and colleges** to budget and to understand basic business concepts to prepare them should they choose to go into business

What advice would she give to other women in a similar position?

- learn as much as you can about business before you venture into it. This is vital
- learn to trust your own instincts and do not allow yourself to be intimidated by agencies, financial advisers and so on
- ensure that the advice you are getting feels appropriate
- above all, do not sink everything into your business. Rebecca and her husband lost everything, including their home. Four years after liquidation they still owe money and nothing much has changed for them

Josephine

Josephine and her partner got into financial difficulties over his business. Although they were in a business partnership as well as living together as a couple, Josephine never regarded the business as hers. Nevertheless they were exhorted to expand and the bank readily agreed to lend them money. All they needed to do was to put their house up as collateral. The business ultimately failed.

Josephine attributes the business failure to the following: they allowed themselves to be swept along the road to 'expansion', which meant borrowing too much money; they allowed themselves to be persuaded by the bank to put the house up as collateral. They had to balance fear of losing the house against investing more money in the business in order to save it.

There were also too many bad debts from too many clients not paying up. This in turn served to increase their debts from around £10,000 to over £100,000 which tipped them into bankruptcy. When the financial climate worsened, the bank demanded its money back. Josephine also blames her own business naïveté – she was not even paid a salary.

What would have helped?

- being properly informed about and aware of the financial and emotional costs of putting the house up as collateral
- feeling as if she had some measure of control over what was happening during these anxious years – which might have helped her to feel that she had an acceptable future

Solicitor's advice

- Josephine had an excellent solicitor who advised her to fight the bank on the grounds that they had not properly advised her of the implications of putting her house up as collateral should the business fail. She was successful in her case against the bank
- a similar case had set a precedent shortly before hers came to court

What advice would she give to other women in a similar position?

- do not put your house up as collateral (as a guarantee) should a business venture fail. There are other ways
- make sure you really understand all the information, the situation and the risks attached. It is *vital* that you understand it all

- try to maintain as far as possible a positive attitude

CPAG's *Debt Advice Handbook* (ch. 14) offers the following advice about business debts: if a business is still trading but has financial difficulties, specialist professional advice should be sought from an accountant, insolvency practitioner, legal business centre or small firms advisory service to determine its viability. Debt advisers, notes Wolfe, often declare themselves unable to deal with a person's debts while they are still running a business.

Types of businesses

Mike Wolfe describes (in the *Debt Advice Handbook*) the various types of business, as these govern the nature of the debtor's liability.

Sole trader

This is someone who is self-employed without business partners, for example electricians, joiners, and so on. S/he is legally responsible for business debts in the same way as you are responsible for personal debts

Partnership

This is a business relationship between two or more people carrying on a business together in order to make a profit. You do not need to have a written formal agreement but it would seem highly advisable in case disputes arise.

A partnership is considered to be a single legal entity so that contracts entered into by any one of the partners normally binds them all – at least while that person is still a member of the partnership. Generally, all partners are equally responsible for all debts accrued during their membership.

Limited companies

This is a means by which a new legal body is set up which can trade to make a profit. This is either kept in the company or distributed to its owners, the shareholders.

Business debts

Responsibility for the losses fall to the company as a whole rather than to the individuals who have set it up.

The limited company can be public – where the shares can be bought and sold on the stock market; or private – where shares are owned and transferred among a limited number of people as allowed by the company's rules.

The shareholders own the companies which are run by their directors, who may also be shareholders. Directors are elected by shareholders and are employees of the company.

Wolfe notes that, unlike a partnership, the directors are not responsible for the debts of a company unless: they have agreed to act as guarantor for some or all of the company's debts; they have acted fraudulently and the company has been liquidated; or they have continued to trade while the company was insolvent.

Cooperatives

Basically, a cooperative can trade for profit without distributing profits to shareholders; it trades as an independent legal entity and therefore protects its members from responsibility for its own debts.

It is vital for debtors to get specialist help

According to CPAG's *Debt Advice Handbook* (p. 293) this could include listing creditors and minimising debts by ceasing trading.

This process may be helped by drawing up a business plan dealing with the incomings and outgoings of the business and including:

- listing all the business assets, e.g. equipment
- listing likely income to the business
- listing payments from the business
- minimising other debts
- listing and maximising income
- listing expenditure
- dealing with priority debts (rates, rent, VAT)
- drawing up a financial statement
- choosing a strategy for non-priority debts

16 Credit cards and credit agreements

Credit cards made their way on to the market in the 1980s and with them a radical new attitude to credit, borrowing and debt that seemed to emphasise only their positive aspects. This was the culture in which Mary grew up, where credit cards were used to buy whatever she wanted and the notion that she could not afford these things was never mentioned.

Mary

Mary became a compulsive shopper. She got her first credit card when she was 20. It was the mid-1980s. A few years later she had twelve credit cards and debts totalling £20,000; she had been sacked from her job at the bank for stealing money and finally had to declare herself bankrupt.

She attributes this in part to: the ease with which she was able to obtain credit; shops and organisations were (and still are) eager to lend money. Many shops offered her an account or charge card to buy goods in their stores. She also applied for and received several additional credit cards.

She found it was easy to spend the money without having to take responsibility for it. Buying goods or services using a credit card (such as Visa or Mastercard) is simple. You make your purchase and then sign an authorisation slip. You then immediately own these goods. The credit card company is invoiced by the trader and you receive a monthly account showing all the purchases you have made and the minimum repayment that is required. This amount is usually 5 per cent of the total balance or a nominal amount such as £5. Interest is added on sums unpaid by a specified date, or immediately for cash withdrawals

Credit cards and credit agreements

using a credit card. Mary said that the interest rates charged by some credit companies were extortionate – about 40 per cent.

Mary also suffered from a lack of personal or professional support. She did not know the appropriate place for getting help, for example the Debt Helpline or CAB (which she thought would not be able to help her), once she realised that she needed it.

Mary said that as a child she always had what she wanted, even when the family was not very well off. She never heard her parents say that they could not afford things. If they did not have the cash, they would buy what they wanted using credit cards. She thought this was normal. Also, her parents never taught her how to deal with problems because they always denied them.

What would have helped?

- **someone to take control** in order to sort out the debts, particularly in the last few years before she was sacked. However, Mary did not seek help from anyone – in fact, she told no one, not even her husband – until she was sacked
- **feeling good about herself without having to resort to spending money** as a means of boosting her self-esteem as well as providing a comfort

What advice would she give to other women in a similar position?

- **get help as soon as possible**. Ring the Debt Helpline. It is confidential and run by trained volunteers. It is also good to talk to someone who does not know you. Helpline volunteers can share the burden of it all if that is what you want; they write and negotiate on your behalf regardless of the size of the debt – a vet's fee you cannot pay or your business going bust. Also they know the law very well so if, for example, a finance company is threatening you with the bailiffs they can advise you that no action can be taken without first obtaining a court order
- **if you think you are a compulsive shopper get help**. Mary recognised her problem by reading about it in a magazine. She found that joining a group was very helpful. It was good to be with others with similar problems and the label of compulsive shopper was useful as a way of

establishing the problem as a psychological one rather than an illness. Counselling helps to access the underlying reasons for your behaviour

- there is definitely **life after bankruptcy.** Going to court was far less traumatic than Mary had thought it would be; in fact, she said she felt immense relief. She had to see an insolvency practitioner who then dealt with all the correspondence relating to her debts and negotiated with the finance companies on her behalf

Mary's self-esteem has been restored by her achievements, and by studying she has secured a place at university. As she says in her story: 'everything is getting better and better and it has nothing to do with money'.

Shopping by credit card

This is on the increase in Britain. The total number of card holders rose last year by 1.7 million to a record 17.7 million, according to the Association of Payment Clearing Services. The number of cards issued is even greater and now totals 29.5 million.

The ease with which we may now shop, and spend, can prove too great a temptation for some people. 'Compulsive spending disorder' (an American term) differs from the occasional 'binge' spending. It is uncontrolled, excessive spending which can often lead to huge debts, family break-up or even prison. The shoppers – both men and women – often have no use for the goods that they buy. According to Sarah Lonsdale in the *Observer* (16 October 1994), the Director of the Portia Trust, a charity that helps non-criminal shoplifters, says that the similarities between this latter group and compulsive shoppers are striking: both are often suffering from anxiety, stress or depression and are seeking some kind of attention. Neither has any real use for the things they acquire. The only real difference is the way in which they acquire things.

Points to remember

- **credit cards will never be the cheapest way to borrow money**, except possibly to obtain credit in the short-term (up to about six weeks) where no interest is charged at all if the account is cleared at the first due date. However, there are often other charges to watch out for

- **it is worth shopping around for the best deal**. Some credit companies offer additional services such as free legal advice should something you buy on credit turn out to be defective, but you may be paying a higher rate than you would elsewhere

- the cheapest way to use a credit card and avoid paying interest is to **pay your bills in full**. You get free credit if there is no fee and an interest-free period – usually for a specified number of days

- **watch out for hidden charges** like late payments, exceeding credit limits and for bounced cheques

- if you are anxious about your ability to continue repayments, **seek professional help**

Research shows that juggling credit card repayments can become an obsession. Money advisers stress that it is important to seek their help as soon as possible and not to borrow more money in an attempt to pay off debts.

Some money advisers suggest that it may be possible to clear debt more cheaply on existing cards by switching to one of the new cards on the market as they offer some reduction on the rates charged elsewhere, but they suggest you exercise caution when doing so. Also, if you are likely to get into debt again in the future, it may be important to consider the interest rate that applies *after* the introductory period rather than being seduced by introductory offers.

It is always better to clear the debt if possible. If, however, you think you might dive in and out of debt, then go for a card with a low interest rate, no fee and an interest-free period.

17 Bankruptcy: three women's experiences

Bankruptcy can end the anxiety of facing huge debts and allow a debtor to make a fresh start. This may be a sensible strategy, especially if the debts cannot be written off and the debtor does not have any available assets or capital; this includes owning a house, as this would usually be sold to pay off creditors. However, it does mean that you cannot set up in business on your own in the next few years and that even after the Bankruptcy Order is discharged (usually three years), you may still owe money (for example, in fines). It is also expensive, costing £265 in 1995 to declare yourself bankrupt.

Mary

Mary felt 'immense relief' at declaring herself bankrupt. Her debts – run up by using her credit cards – totalled around £20,000. She was advised to go to court and plead bankruptcy. She was subsequently discharged of all responsibility for her debts and the court appointed an insolvency adviser who took over all future correspondence and negotiation in relation to these debts. This was a turning point for her. The help she received through the court enabled her to begin to deal with her life in a different and more positive way.

Rebecca

Rebecca, on the other hand, is still mortified by her business collapse because so many people suffered as a result. Some creditors went unpaid, former employees have been unable to find further work and she and her husband, as well as her investor, lost a tremendous amount of money as well as their home. The experience has also badly affected the whole family. Rebecca likens losing the business to a bereavement. Several years after liquidation they still owe money and there seems little respite from the nightmare.

Josephine

Josephine and her partner lived together and set up a business, putting up their house as collateral. The business eventually collapsed, largely because many of their clients ended up not paying them. Although this was a partnership and technically they were both responsible for the business debts, Josephine's solicitor was successful in bringing a case against the bank which loaned them the money on the grounds that she was not properly informed of the consequences of putting her home up as collateral at the time of the loan. Josephine's main fear was that she was going to lose the house. Several years later, after going into voluntary liquidation, she was able to buy the house back from the bank for a comparatively small amount of money.

The Citizens' Advice Bureau in Bristol has published *A Positive Approach to Dealing with Your Debts* and advises that if you have large debts and you cannot come to suitable repayment arrangements with your creditors, or if you will not be able to pay the debt in the foreseeable future, you may wish to think about bankruptcy. This can be a good way to wipe the slate clean and make a fresh start.

Bankruptcy can have serious consequences and you should get advice before going ahead. (For further discussion see CPAG's *Debt Advice Handbook*, ch. 13.)

The Insolvency Service within the Department of Trade and Industry has produced *A Guide to Bankruptcy* which explains what bankruptcy means, what happens if you are made bankrupt in England and Wales, and gives information about some of the (cheaper) alternatives to bankruptcy, for example an Administration Order made by the county court (provided your debts do not exceed £5,000 and you are in a position to make regular payments). There may also be the option of an Individual

Voluntary Arrangement where you make a formal proposal to your creditors through the court to pay all or part of your debts. Any agreement reached with your creditors would be binding on them. This booklet is available at Citizens' Advice Bureaux.

18 Being a student

'The present system of financial support for students is chaotic, inequitable and inefficient' (Official Report, House of Lords, 30 January 1995 c1313).

There are now more students in higher education than ever before; nearly one in every three young people enters higher education compared with one in eight in 1979. However, poverty and the prospect of financial hardship are driving down the number of university applicants. Growing numbers of students are contemplating having to give up, or have already given up, their university courses because of financial hardship.

Most students are no longer entitled to Income Support, Housing Benefit or Unemployment Benefit while they are on a full-time course and including vacations (although the regulations do not spell out a definition of full-time). Single parents are stated as being the exception: they are still entitled to Income Support, but only if they have a child under 16 living with them; this means that they are therefore exempt from the availability-to-work rule. However, the income calculated from a student loan – which most people are obliged to take out – means that many do not ultimately qualify for Income Support. Also, unless they have a loan they cannot get financial help from the university's hardship fund. And you cannot get a loan unless you are aged under 50.

Isobel

Isobel, a mature student whose story appears in this book, is aged 55. She would have benefited from one of the very few allowances for which she was eligible – the Mature Students' Allowance – but it was abolished in September 1995 in spite of research that shows the greater financial hardship of older students.

Single-parent students like Isobel therefore begin their courses potentially under great financial strain and have to bear the burden of a system that ostensibly appears to help those most in need, but is in fact intent on reducing public funding and increasingly supporting a system of private-sector loans.

Isobel's life as a student was dominated by lack of money. She was divorced about eight years ago, after 25 years of marriage. She has three dependent children. They have all become university students themselves and have also been plagued by lack of money as students. Their grants have been inadequate to meet their needs. The children's father has never supported them financially although he earns a good salary and so does his partner.

Isobel attributes her inability to manage her finances to various factors. These include the following: the grant was totally inadequate to meet her needs; she already had debts before becoming a student, although most of these were her ex-husband's; and she needed to buy lots of books because of her disabilities.

Isobel felt unable to deal head-on with her debts and was hampered by lack of financial support from her ex-husband even though she had helped him to get through university when they were married.

What would have helped?

- **seeking advice earlier**. She had access to a financial adviser at university
- having **help with emotional difficulties** so that she felt more supported, especially in the community
- some **positive financial discrimination** because of her disabilities
- getting **more financial help by way of grants** – for example, travel grant, bursaries for the extra books she needed – and for this help to be easily accessible rather than difficult and complicated
- if she had not been denied a student loan (because she was over 50) she would also have been eligible to apply to the **hardship fund**

- **being aware that she could have applied for various grants** and other charities
- **someone to take responsibility for managing the debts**, especially the house which she thought was going to be repossessed

What advice would she give to other women in a similar position?

- **do not take on too much**, especially if you have financial as well as other problems. Isobel found that the anxiety of doing so affected her study profoundly. She found it difficult to concentrate and as a result she felt she achieved only half her potential
- **get professional help** sooner rather than later

Isobel has her degree. If she had calculated the cost of this before she started she would probably not have embarked on a university course at all. Ultimately she thinks it was worth taking the risk.

Financial facts about being a student

A student may get his or her course fees paid (these are paid direct to the institution) and receive a student grant which is calculated according to a means test. The grant includes a basic maintenance allowance during term time, Christmas and Easter holidays. Extra allowances may be available for students with disabilities, for some travel, and for special circumstances such as a couple having to maintain two homes while one partner attends his/her course. There are also students' dependants allowances which are means-tested, and the single-parent allowance.

Student loans were introduced in 1990. These loans are administered through the Student Loan Company and are a cheaper form of long-term borrowing than banks. Loans are not means-tested and are paid in instalments according to what suits the student best.

Check the amount which parents are expected to contribute to their student children's maintenance. There are many exceptions. The amount is stated on the grant notification.

A NatWest Bank survey in 1995 indicated that the average level of debt for students aged 17 to 21 was £2,500. The same survey also found that 50 per cent of debt was due to accommodation costs.

With the introduction of loans instead of grants, as well as maintenance and tuition fees it is estimated that before long a typical student will be leaving university with debts of £20,000 or more.

If you have dropped out of your course or been dismissed, then you can claim benefit from that date. If you are studying part-time you may be eligible for benefit, provided your course lasts no more than 21 hours a week and you are prepared to take a job if a suitable one comes up.

Discretionary payments from access funds are administered by the institutions themselves 'who have discretion to make payments to those whose education might be inhibited by financial constraints' (Department of Social Security Policy Branch). However, you have to be in receipt of a loan in order to claim help from the access or hardship fund. Contact the financial adviser who should help you to make the application.

Hardship funds and additional funds such grants or interest-free loans may be available to help students in financial difficulties. Contact your student union or student services department.

If students take up part of a loan, then those who are eligible for benefits will have £10 a week ignored in their calculation for entitlement to Income Support and Housing Benefit.

An increasing number of students are forced to find work in term time and in the holidays and this affects the quality of their study.

There are charities available which will consider giving financial help to students. You are more likely to succeed if you are near the end of your course and/or where funding arrangements have broken down.

Financial facts for graduates

Debts are forcing graduates to take the first available job and deterring them from seeking further qualifications, according to a survey by the University Careers Service. More than two-thirds of the 5,000 questioned were graduating with debts between £3,000 and £10,000, adding to pressure to take low-paid work ('Great Expectations: the new diversity of graduate skills and aspirations').

Being a student

Graduates can sign on for Income Support of up to £37.90 per week as soon as the term has officially ended. Some will also be entitled to Housing Benefit if they are paying rent.

Should you be lucky enough to get a job, make sure you avoid the hassle of being put on an emergency tax code and then having to claim it back. If you do not expect to earn more than your personal allowance – you can earn up to £3,765 a year tax-free – ask your local tax office for form P38(S) and give it to your employer.

Most banks offer graduates – both employed and unemployed – loans of up to £5,000 and interest-free overdrafts to help them during their job search. They will also provide low-rate graduate loans to help prepare you for work; for example to purchase suitable clothes or a car. Most are also willing to extend the interest-free period on overdrafts while graduates find their feet.

It is important to remember that loans from the Student Loan Company are a cheaper form of long-term borrowing. Students can defer repayment after graduation so long as their income remains below 85 per cent of average earnings. Interest continues to be charged during any period of deferment.

Repayment of the student loan is enforceable through the county courts. Recovery of debt to the institution – for example, tuition fees – varies, but some will not allow the student to continue. While this action may be lawful it is likely to be unlawful to prevent a student from continuing his studies where certain other debts are outstanding – for example, accommodation fees or library fines.

If the bank offers to convert your overdraft to a loan, make sure it has a deferred repayment arrangement otherwise you could find yourself in further debt and unable to keep up these repayments. Do not feel pressured into accepting loan arrangements offered by banks.

CPAG's *Debt Advice Handbook* (p. 321) advises that a student will often be better off by ceasing to use an existing bank account and using an ordinary building society savers' account, even though it will mean the loss of the interest-free overdraft facility.

See also, 'Student Loans as a Guide for Students', Student Loans Company Ltd, 100 Bothwell Street, Glasgow G2 7JD; and 'Student Grants and Loans – a brief guide for higher education students', published annually by the Department of Further Education and available from LEAs and colleges.

Resources

Bankruptcy

The ordeal of bankruptcy affects 30,000 people each year in the UK. John McQueen, founder of the **Bankruptcy Association of Great Britain and Ireland**, has produced a practical guide to the insolvency laws. The organisation was set up in 1983 and offers help and advice to members who pay £15 a year to join. It has helped thousands of people. John McQueen's book, *Bankruptcy Explained*, costs £7.95 (available from the Bankruptcy Association, TEL 01482 658 701).

A cheaper alternative is to reach a repayment agreement through direct negotiation with the creditors. CABx, solicitors, accountants and local money advice agencies will sometimes negotiate with creditors on the debtor's behalf although in many cases bankruptcy cannot be avoided.

The Department of Trade and Industry has produced *A Guide to Bankruptcy*. It explains what bankruptcy means, what happens if you are made bankrupt in England or Wales and some of the possible, cheaper alternatives to bankruptcy.

Carers

The Carers' National Association is a charity set up to help Britain's seven million carers. One of its main concerns is that thousands of people who care for sick or disabled individuals are missing out on much-needed state benefits. Their **Caring for Carers Campaign** offers a free helpline enabling carers to find out if they are eligible for financial help. TEL (freephone) 0800 100 000 between 10 a.m. and 4 p.m. weekdays.

Children

The Child Poverty Action Group unfortunately cannot deal with enquiries direct from the public but advisers can phone the advice line which is open from 2 p.m. to 4 p.m. Monday to Thursday (TEL 0171 253 6569) or write to CPAG at Citizens' Rights Office CPAG, 4th Floor, 1–5 Bath Street, London EC1V 9PY. CPAG can take up a limited number of complex cases, including appeals to the child support commissioners or court, if referred by an adviser. CPAG is continuing to monitor the implementation of legislation and to lobby for changes, so please notify them of any case that demonstrates a difficulty, anomaly or delay, or where hardship has been caused by the child support scheme. For a list of their publications, see 'Useful publications', p. 205, available by phoning 0171 253 3406.

Child Support Agency (CSA). It is not usually possible as an individual to make contact direct with the CSA. The following organisations can help: Citizens' Advice Bureaux or other local advice centres; law centres; solicitors can give free legal advice under the green form scheme (pink form in Scotland); welfare rights workers attached to your local authority.

If you feel you have been dealt with unfairly by the CSA, the Child Poverty Action Group would like to hear from you.

Compulsive shopping

Wallet Watch was set up by a compulsive shopper to help others with the same problem. The group can be contacted by writing to 61 Whitehouse Way, Southgate, London N14 7LX.

The **Portia Trust** is a charity offering help to 'non-criminal' shoplifters. Telephone 01889 507 510 for further details, advice or support.

Credit

Credit Unions have emerged in recent years as one of the most effective weapons against loan sharks (money lenders who charge crippling interest rates). Their aim is to help people clear debts without resorting to loans. You may become a Union member and pay regular amounts to a non-profit-making pool instead of trying to meet weekly payments to money lenders. Contact your local CAB to see if there is a Credit Union in your area.

Debt

Debtors Anonymous This is a self-supporting group and membership is free. It is described as a 'fellowship of men and women who share their experience, strength and hope with each other, that they may solve their common problem and help others to recover from compulsive debting. The only requirement is the desire to stop incurring unsecured debt.' For meetings, telephone 0142 694 7150 (answering machine).

Disability

If you have been disabled through an accident or a criminal act you may qualify for a range of benefits. Most are means-tested, including Income Support, Housing Benefit, Council Tax Benefit, Disability Working Allowance and grants from the Independent Living Fund. Those not means-tested include Incapacity Benefit, Disability Living Allowance, Attendance Allowance, Severe Disablement Allowance and payments from the Industrial Injuries Scheme. Further information is available from the **Disablement Income Group**, Unit 5, Archway Business Centre, 19–23 Wedmore Street, London N19 4RZ, TEL 0171 263 3981.

Chase de Vere Investments has a leaflet on how to find a suitable independent financial adviser. For a free copy write to Chase de Vere, 63 Lincoln Inn Fields, London WC2A 3JX, TEL 0800 526 091.

Radar is a national voluntary organisation which represents all those with a physical disability. It campaigns on behalf of physically disabled people, produces fact sheets on education, holidays, employment and mobility as well as various publications including benefits and civil rights. It is also involved in administering the national key scheme. There are regional offices throughout the country. Telephone 0171 250 3222 to find your nearest office.

Divorce

The **Solicitors' Family Law Association** is a group of solicitors committed to a conciliatory approach to family law.

Fairshares is an organisation set up in 1993 to campaign for a fairer deal for spouses, particularly wives, regarding the automatic entitlement to a share in their husbands' pensions in divorce settlements. It is a self-help group actively involved in campaigning. It produces a regular newsletter. For further details contact Dawn Barnet, 14 Park Road, Rugby, Warwickshire CV21 2QH, TEL 01788 570585.

Drugs

Contact the **National Drugs Helpline** (0800 776600) for free, confidential 24-hour advice, or simply to talk.

Homelessness

Shelter is a housing charity campaigning for the homeless. Their offices give help to people looking for accommodation: TEL 0171 253 0202.

CABx and council welfare rights departments also give free advice.

Maternity benefits

For information about maternity benefits, send a stamped addressed envelope to the **Maternity Alliance**, 45 Beech Street, London EC2P 2LX.

There is also a booklet, 'Maternity Rights' (Ref PL958), available from CABx, libraries or jobcentres or from Cambertown, Unit 8, Commercial Road, Goldthorpe, Rotherham S63 9BL, TEL 01709 888 688.

Money

The Money Advice Association is a national organisation set up to provide advice to people in debt.

The Money Advice Trust is a charity whose debtline employs experienced debt advisers who can help callers negotiate realistic repayment terms with creditors, including freezing interest on what is owed so that debts do not continue to mount. In exceptional circumstances it can arrange for the debt to be written off completely. TEL 0121 359 8501.

Redundancy

It pays to take advice as soon as you suspect that you might lose your job. Contact your trade union, CAB, Law Centre or solicitor but ensure that they specialise in employment law. The **Employment Lawyers Association** specialises in employment law. Tel 01895 256 972.

Redundancy Handling is a free booklet available from ACAS (the Advisory, Conciliation and Arbitration Service) to check that your employers have done everything correctly. If you think you have been unfairly treated, get advice immediately. You may be able to bring a claim for unfair dismissal.

Sex industry

The **Bethany Project** is a charitable organisation set up recently for women who want to leave the sex industry, including women who have exchanged sex for money, drugs or alcohol and are in need of support. It provides a safe, women-only environment to explore underlying issues. You will be required to pay some expenses from your benefits. The house is drug- and alcohol-free. Bethany is in the Manchester area but accepts referrals nationally. There is no need for a care in the community assessment. Unfortunately the building is not suitable for children. TEL 0161 445 1311.

Single parents

The following organisations can offer help and advice about child support: **Gingerbread** (telephone 0171 240 0953 for details about your local group); **Single Parent Action Network** (TEL 0117 051 4231); **National Council for One-Parent Families** (TEL 0171 267 1361); **Scottish Council for Single Parents** (TEL 0131 556 3899).

Small businesses

Help on how to start setting up a small business is offered by **Lawyers for Your Business**. This is a free service offered by the Law Society. Ring 0171 405 9075 for an explanatory leaflet, a list of participating solicitors in your area and a voucher to claim a free half-hour interview.

The **Business Link** provides access to all local business support agencies, including the Training and Enterprise Council, the Local Enterprise Agency, the Chamber of Commerce and your local authority. TEL 0700 405060.

Other useful contacts include: **Federation of Small Businesses**, TEL 0171 233 7900; **Forum of Private Business**, TEL 01565 634467.

Students

Students may wish to study the 'Student Loans as a Guide for Students' which can be obtained from the **Student Loans Company**, 100 Bothwell Street, Glasgow G2 7JD. Another guide published annually by the Department of Further Education is 'Student Grants and Loans – a brief guide for higher education students', available from local education authorities and colleges.

Useful organisations

Benefits Agency Chief Executive
Mr P. Mathison
Quarry House
Quarry Hill
Leeds LS2 7UA
TEL 0113 232 4000

Child Support Appeals Tribunals
CSAT's Central Office
8th Floor Anchorage 2
Anchorage Quay
Salford Quays M5 2YN
TEL 0345 626 311

Consumer Credit Association
Queen's House
Queen's Road
Chester CH1 3BQ
TEL 01244 312 044

Council for Mortgage Lenders (CML)
3 Savile Row
London W1X 1AF
TEL 0171 437 0655

Disability Appeals Tribunals
DAT's Central Office
PO Box 168
Nottingham NG1 5JX
TEL 0345 247 246

Disability Working Allowance Unit
Diadem House
1 The Pavilion
Preston PR2 2GN
TEL 01772 883300

DSS Solicitor
New Court
48 Carey Street
London WC2A 2LS
TEL 0171 962 8000

Family Credit Unit
Government Buildings
Warbreck Hill Road
Blackpool FY2 0AX
TEL 01253 500050

Health Service Ombudsman
Millbank Tower
London SW1P 4QP

Income-Support (16–17-year-olds)
Severe Hardship Claims Unit
174 Pitt Street
Glasgow G2 4DZ
TEL 0141 225 4259

Independent Review Service for the Social Fund
4th Floor, Centre City Podium
5 Hill Street
Birmingham B5 4UB
TEL 0121 606 2100

Maternity Alliance
45 Beech Street
London EC2P 2LX
TEL 0171 588 8582

Money Advice Association
1st Floor, Gresham House
24 Holborn Viaduct

London EC1A 2BN
TEL 0171 236 3566

Money Advice Scotland
Strathclyde Regional Council
MATRU
85 Parnie Street
Glasgow GL1 5RQ
TEL 0141 552 3402

National Association of Citizens' Advice Bureaux
115–123 Pentonville Road
London N1 9LZ
TEL 0171 833 2181

National Consumer Council
20 Grosvenor Gardens
London SW1W 0DH
TEL 0171 730 3469

National Council for One-Parent Families
255 Kentish Town Road
London NW5 2LX
TEL 0171 267 1361

National Debtline
TEL 0121 359 8501
(Also see 'Money' in Resources Section, p. 197)

National Federation of Credit Unions
Units 1.1 and 1.2, Howard Place
Commercial Centre
Howard Street
North Shields NE30 1AR
TEL 0191 257 2219

Office of the Ombudsman for Health and the Parliamentary Commissioner (for England)
Church House
Great Smith Street
London SW1P 3BW
TEL 0171 276 3000

Office of the Pension Ombudsman
11 Belgrave Road
London WIV 1RB
TEL 0171 834 9144

Social Security Appeals Tribunals
Mr R. Hubbins, National Chairperson
39–45 Finsbury Square
London EC2A 1PX
TEL 0171 814 6500 for your Regional Chairperson

Many of the above organisations give advice. If you are in dispute with the Benefits Agencies about your entitlements or have financial difficulties and are unable to keep up payments, it may be better to seek independent advice from one of the following (listed in CPAG's *National Welfare Benefits Handbook*, Appendix 3):

- **Citizens' Advice Bureaux** (CABx) provide information and advice about benefits and may be able to represent you
- **Law Centres** also provide similar help
- **local authority welfare rights workers** provide a service in many areas. Some arrange advice sessions and take up campaigns locally
- **local organisations** for particular groups of claimants may offer help; for example, there are unemployment centres, pensioners' groups, centres for people with disabilities
- **Claimants' Unions** give advice in some areas. Contact the Plymouth Claimants' Union, PO Box 21, Plymouth PL1 1QS or the Swindon Unemployed Movement, Room 20, Pinehurst People's Centre, Beech Avenue, Pinehurst, Swindon, Wiltshire.
- some **social workers and probation officers** (but not all) help with benefits, especially if they are already working with you on another problem
- **solicitors** can give free legal advice under the green form scheme (pink form in Scotland) although it is important to find a solicitor who has a good working knowledge of the benefit rules

- **Refugee Council**, 3 Bond Way, London SW8 1SJ
- **Joint Council for the Welfare of Immigrants**, 115 Old Bond Street, London EC1V 9JR

You can obtain free telephone advice on benefits on the following numbers (general advice and specific queries on individual claims):
Benefits Enquiry Line 0800 666555
Enquiry line for people with disabilities 0800 882 200
Family Credit Helpline 01253 500 050 (this is not a freephone line); Northern Ireland 0800 616 757
Advice is available in the following languages:

- Cantonese 0800 252 451
- Punjabi 0800 521 360
- Urdu 0800 289 188
- Welsh 0800 289 011

Useful Publications

Books

Child Support Handbook (CPAG)
Council Tax Handbook, Martin Ward (CPAG)
Council Tax Housing (SHAC and CPAG)
Debt Advice Handbook, Mike Wolfe (CPAG)
Disability Rights Handbook (Disability Alliance ERA)
Fuel Rights Handbook, Hoffland and Nicol (CPAG)
Guide to Community Charge, Martin Ward (Zebedee Institute of Housing)
Income-Related Benefits: The Legislation, Mesher (CPAG)
Jobseekers Allowance Handbook, Richard Poynter (CPAG)
Medical and Disability Appeal Tribunals: The Legislation, Mark Rowland (CPAG)
National Welfare Benefits Handbook (CPAG)
Rights Guide for Homeowners (CPAG and Shelter)
Rights Guide to Non-Means-Tested Benefits (CPAG)
The Social Fund: Law and Practice, Trevor Buck (CPAG)
Unemployment and Training Rights Handbook (Unemployment Unit)
Welfare Rights Bulletin (CPAG) (Bi-monthly update for welfare rights advisers)

Most of these books are available in the reference section of public libraries or from Child Poverty Action Group Ltd, 4th Floor, 1–5 Bath Street, London EC1V 9PY, TEL 0171 253 3406.

Leaflets

The Department of Social Security publishes leaflets covering particular benefits or groups of claimants. They are free, detailed and informative and may be obtained at your local DSS office or from DSS Information Division, Leaflets Unit, Block 4, Government Buildings, Honeypot Lane, Stanmore, Middlesex HA7 1AY.

Index

Access Funds, at universities 61, 62
addiction *see* compulsive shopping; drug addiction
addiction model of debt survival 13
additional personal allowance 159, 170, 172–3
advice
　about benefits 137
　lacking in Jennifer's case 32–3
　on maximum income 134
　see also professional advice
advice agencies
　criticisms of 16
　help from 121–2, 128
alcohol abuse 22, 24–5, 43, 44, 46, 47, 108
anger, impact of business failure 87, 88
anxiety 11–12, 23–4
　Alice's case 56–7, 92–3
appeals and reviews 156, 175
attitudes to money and debt 14–16, 19
　influence of background on 15–16, 117–18
　Laura's story 34, 35, 37, 40
　Lisa's story 68
　Margaret's story 103
　Mary's story 113, 117–18, 120
avoidance 9–10, 63, 115
　see also secrecy

babies *see* children

baby break pensions 153
back-to-work bonuses 138
bank loans
　for businesses 79, 85–6, 178
　houses as collateral 90, 94–5, 97–8, 179, 187
　for graduates 193
　Margaret's story 107
　Mary's story 114
bankruptcy 184, 186
　help and information 187–8, 194
　Jennifer's story 30
　Josephine's story 90, 91, 94, 187
　Laura's story 38
　Mary's story 121, 184, 186
　Rebecca's story 85–9, 186–7
Bankruptcy Association of Great Britain and Ireland 194
banks
　attitudes to businesses 85–6
　attitudes to women in business 77–8, 95
　embezzlement 116, 117, 118
　inadequate information from 89, 94–5, 98, 131, 179, 187
　overdrafts 66, 193
battered wives *see* violence within marriage
benefits *see* state benefits
Benefits Agency
　payment of mortgage by 143
　see also Department of Social Security
Bethany Project 198

206

Index

budgeting loans 146–7
building societies *see* mortgage payments
bursaries, at universities 61
business
  anxiety over failure of 92–3
  attitudes to women in 5–6, 77–8, 80–1, 85, 95
  grants for 79–80
  help and information for 198–9
  impact on children and relationships 87, 88, 91, 92, 95, 97
  investment in Rebecca's 84–5
  Josephine's involvement in 90, 91, 95–6
  knowledge of 78–9, 86
  maternal management style 81–2
  problems of small-scale 78
  starting 77–8, 85
  training and marketing 82–3
  types of 180–1
  see also bank loans; enterprise and development agencies
business debts
  bankruptcy 186–7
  coping with 181
  Josephine's story 15, 90–1, 95–6, 178–80, 187
  liability for 180–1
  Rebecca's story 85, 86, 87, 177–8, 186
Business Link 198–9

CAB (Citizens' Advice Bureau) 128
carers, help and information for 194
Carers National Association 194
charge cards 130
charging orders 30, 169
Chase de Vere Investments 196
Child Benefit 8, 45, 158–9
child care 14, 170
child maintenance 171–2
  Isobel's story 60, 65
  non-payment of 40–1, 43–4, 68–9, 75–6, 159, 160, 168–9
  see also Child Support Agency
Child Poverty Action Group (CPAG) 195
Child Support Agency (CSA) 165–9, 195
  client dissatisfaction with 13, 159, 169
  functions of 165
  Laura's story 40–1, 159
  power of 167–8
  procedures to retrieve payments 168–9
children
  costs of having 149
  custody in Emily's case 45
  effects of businesses on 88, 97
  help and information regarding 195
  impact of debt on 31, 73, 154
  impact on women's earning power 13–14
  Margaret's story 101–2, 105–7, 108
  responsibility for 158–9
  see also maternity payments; maternity rights; parenthood
Citizen's Advice Bureau (CAB) 128
clean-break settlements 56, 164
cohabitation
  and eligibility for Income Support 155
  reviews and appeals 156
community workers 75
compulsive shopping
  counselling for and talking about 119, 122
  extent of 112
  help and information regarding 183–4, 195
  link with self-esteem and power 113, 119–20

compulsive shopping *contd*
  Mary's story 112, 119, 122, 182–4
    reasons for shopping 113
    research on 112
    treatment of 112
    see also credit cards and agreements
Consumer Credit Act (1974) 129
contracts, validity of 131–2
contractual maternity pay 150
control
  link with coping 127
  Margaret's experience of debt and 109
  need for others to take control 39, 116, 117, 183
  see also independence
cooperatives, and liability for debts 181
coping strategies
  and degree of control 127
  meditation 96
  positive visualisation 95
  see also surviving debt
counselling, for compulsive shopping 122
CPAG (Child Poverty Action Group) 195
credit cards and agreements
  ease of obtaining 113–14, 182
  features of credit cards 184–5
  help and information regarding 195–6
  Margaret's story 103, 106
  Mary's story 112–13, 182–4
  shopping by credit card 182, 184
  switching cards 185
Credit Unions 195–6
credit-related debts 129–30
creditors, licensing of 132–3
crises
  emergency aid for 128
  help for parents from social services 154

crisis loans 138, 147
CSA *see* Child Support Agency

debt
  addiction model 13
  consolidation into single loan 128, 185
  economic background to 4
  extent of 4
  help and information regarding 196, 197–8
  inaccuracies regarding 132–3
  issues for women 5–8, 13–19
  meaning of being in debt 3–5
  as metaphor for life 20
  PTSD model of survival 8–12
  reasons and triggers for debt crises 4–5, 127, 129
  secrecy and collusion 35–6, 37, 39, 40, 109, 114–15, 116
  self-help for women 16–17, 111
  trauma caused by 4
  types of 129–30
  validity of and liability for 130–3
  and women's employment position 13–14
  see also attitudes to money and debt; business debts; surviving debt
Debt Helpline 120–2, 183
Debtors Anonymous 196
deduction from earnings orders 168
Department of Social Security (DSS)
  categorization of couple 156–7
  Jennifer's experience with 29, 32, 33
  Lisa's experience with 71
  loans and grants from 7, 138, 146–8
  see also Benefits Agency; state benefits

Index

depression 11–12, 56, 64, 71, 74, 119
  see also suicide
development agencies *see* enterprise and development agencies
disability
  help and information regarding 196
  Isobel's story 61, 62, 64–5
Disability Allowance 64
Disability Working Allowance 175–6
Disablement Income Group 196
discrimination
  against single mothers 75
  due to pregnancy 152
  see also paternalism; prejudice
dismissal
  Mary's story 116, 118
  of pregnant women 151–2
distress warrants 168–9
divorce
  Alice's story 51, 54–6, 57–8, 160–2
  clean-break settlements 56, 164
  Emily's story 46, 47
  help and information regarding 196–7
  impact on women 14
  importance of positive outcome 164–5
  Isobel's story 59, 60, 61, 65
  and traditional role of women 50–1, 163–4
  see also Child Support Agency; pensions; separation
drug addiction
  extent of 99
  Margaret's story 99, 102–9
  treatment 109–11
drugs, help and information regarding 197
DSS *see* Department of Social Security

economic background to debt problems 4

education *see* students
electricity bills 63–4
embezzlement 116, 117, 118
emergency appointments with CAB 128
employment
  benefits for parents on low pay 174–6
  boosting women's self-confidence 81–2
  help for homeowners on low incomes 142
  Mary's dismissal 116, 118
  maternity rights 151–2
  women's patterns of 13–14
  see also maternity payments; redundancy; unemployment
Employment Lawyers Association 137, 198
enterprise and development agencies 79–80, 88, 177–8, 198–9
eviction 43

Fairshares 50, 54–5, 197
families
  changing patterns 13
  role of women *see* traditional role of women
Family Credit 174–6
fear of losing home 93–4
Federation of Small Businesses 199
finance companies 114
financial advisers 127–8
fines, imprisonment for non-payment of 6–7, 8
Forum of Private Business 199

garnishee orders 169
Gingerbread 199
graduates 66, 192–3
grants
  for businesses 79–80
  from DSS 7–8, 146
  maternity grants 106, 151
  see also student grants

grievance procedures, and disputes over SMP 152
guilt 10
  and collapse of Rebecca's business 10–11, 86, 87, 88
  Jennifer's feelings of 11
  Josephine's story 95
  Margaret's feelings of 11
  and self-blame in Laura's case 39–40
  and shame in Mary's case 118, 119

harassment, law regarding 133
helplessness, feelings of 62, 109
higher education *see* students
homelessness, help and information regarding 197
house repossession
  flexible approach to 142
  Isobel's fear of 63
  Jennifer's story 21, 28, 30, 33, 139–41
  Josephine's story 91, 93–4, 96–7, 98
  statistics 141
household budgeting 7–8, 16, 23
houses
  as collateral for loans 90, 94–5, 97–8, 179, 187
  Isobel's half-share 64
  Rebecca's loss of 86
housewives *see* traditional role of women
Housing Benefit 40–1
housing market, collapse of 4

imprisonment, for non-payment of fines 6–7, 8
income
  benefits for parents on low pay 174–6
  help for homeowners on low incomes 142
  means of maximising 134, 170

Income Support 138
  and Child Benefit 158–9
  Jennifer's story 28, 32–3
  and mortgage payments 143–5
  separation and eligibility for 155, 157
  for single parents 28, 32–3, 166–7, 170
  for students 189
  see also Jobseeker's Allowance
independence
  Josephine's story 91
  Laura's story 41–2
  lost in Alice's case 52–3
  lost and regained in Emily's case 45, 46–8, 49–50
  Margaret's attitude to 100
  regained in Mary's case 121
  see also control
Individual Voluntary Arrangements 187–8
Invalidity Allowance 64

Jobseeker's Allowance (JSA) 137–8

Lawyers for your Business 198
letters, responses to debt-related letters 10, 62–3, 73, 115
liability, for debts 130–3, 180–1
liability orders 168
limited companies, and liability for debts 180–1
liquidation *see* bankruptcy
loan sharks 131
loans
  consolidation of debts into single loan 128, 185
  from DSS 146
    budgeting loans 146–7
    crisis loans 138, 147
    repayment of 147–8
    Social Fund 7, 138, 147
  from finance companies 114
  see also bank loans; student loans
lone parent premium 170

Index

maintenance 171–2
  Alice's case 55, 56, 160
  Isobel's story 60, 65
  non-payment of 40–1, 43–4, 68–9, 75–6, 159, 160, 168–9
  see also Child Support Agency
maintenance bonuses 167
marketing, Rebecca's business 79–80, 82–3
marriage contracts 164–5
Maternity Alliance 197
Maternity Allowance 150, 151
maternity expenses, for single parents 171
maternity grants 106, 151
maternity leave 149, 151, 152
maternity payments
  contractual maternity pay 150
  disputes about 152–3
  from Social Fund 170
  how to claim 151, 171
  information regarding 197
  Maternity Allowance 150, 151
  statutory maternity pay (SMP) 149–50, 151, 152–3
maternity rights 151–2
mature students
  grants for 59
  Isobel's story 59–67, 189–91
  Lisa's story 68–73
Mature Student's Allowance 189–90
means-tested benefits 134–5
mediation, and divorce 162
meditation, as coping technique 96
methadone 105, 106
money
  help and information regarding 197–8
  see also attitudes to money and debt
Money Advice Association 197
Money Advice Trust 197–8
mortgage payments
  dealing with job loss and 143
  flexibility for parents 153–4
  flexible approaches to arrears 21–2, 141–2
  help for home owners on low incomes 142
  and Income Support 143–5
  Jennifer's story 21, 25, 28, 29–31, 33, 139–41
  payment protection policies 145
  see also house repossession

National Council for One-Parent Families 199
National Drugs Helpline 197
non-means-tested benefits 135–6

one parent benefit 170
overdrafts 66, 193

parenthood
  benefits for parents on low pay 174–6
  help from social services departments 71, 154
  maternity rights 151–2
  suspension of payments 153–4
  see also Child Support Agency; children; maternity payments; single parents
partnerships, and liability for debts 180
paternalism, attitudes to women in business 6, 77–8, 80, 95
payment protection policies on mortgages 145
pensions
  Alice's divorce 55, 58, 160–1, 163
  baby break pensions 153
  dividing assets on divorce 50, 161, 162–3
  'earmarking' 50, 161, 163

implication of maternity
    leave for 151
  splitting of 50
Pensions Act 50
Portia Trust 195
post-traumatic stress disorder
    (PTSD) model 8–12
poverty, as result of debt 7
pregnancy *see* maternity
    payments; maternity rights
prejudice
  against single parents 75
  against women in business
    80
  attitudes to women and
    money 5, 6, 80
  see also discrimination;
    paternalism
professional advice 127
  advertising agencies 82–3
  incorrect in Jennifer's case
    31, 32
  see also banks; solicitors
psychic numbing as response to
    debt 10
PTSD (post-traumatic stress
    disorder) model 8–12

Radar 196
redundancy 137, 198
relationships
  impact of business on 87, 91,
    92, 95
  see also divorce; separation
rent arrears 43, 106
repossession *see* house
    repossession
reviews and appeals 156, 175

Scottish Council for Single
    Parents 199
secrecy
  and collusion in Laura's case
    35–6, 37, 39, 40
  Margaret's story 109
  Mary's story 114–15, 116
self-confidence
  boosting women's 81–2

Josephine's loss of 95
  Lisa's lack of 70–1
self-esteem and self-worth
  and divorce 163–4
  Laura's lack of 36
  link with shopping 113,
    119–20
  loss of 10
  Margaret's lack of 104–5
  regained in Emily's case 48, 49
  regained in Mary's case 184
  role of drugs in boosting 102
self-help, for women in debt
    16–17, 111
separation
  DSS categorization of couple
    156–7
  and eligibility for Income
    Support 155, 157
  Jennifer's story 26–7
  Laura's story 38–42, 159–60,
    169
  Lisa's story 68–9, 75–6
  and reconciliation in Emily's
    case 44, 46, 47–8
  and responsibility for
    children 158–9
  see also Child Support
    Agency; divorce
sex industry, help to leave 198
shame
  Mary's story 118, 119
  see also guilt
Shelter 197
shopping *see* compulsive
    shopping; credit cards and
    agreements
Single Parent Action Network
    199
single parents
  cuts in benefits to 8
  help and information for 199
  Isobel's experience of being a
    student 60, 65, 66, 190
  Lisa's experience of being a
    student 68–76
  maximising income 170–3
  as students 189

Index

SMP *see* statutory maternity pay
Social Fund 7, 138, 147, 151
social security *see* Department of Social Security
social services departments 45–6, 71, 154
sole traders, and liability for debts 180
solicitors
  dealing with 161–2
  poor advice
    on damages in Isobel's case 64–5
    on divorce in Alice's case 50, 51, 56, 58, 160–1, 163
    on divorce in Jennifer's case 26
Solicitors' Family Law Association 196
state benefits 134–6
  Child Benefit 8, 45, 158–9
  Disability Allowances 64, 175–6
  Family Credit 174–6
  Jobseeker's Allowance 137–8
  for parents on low pay 174–6
  reviews and appeals 156, 175
  for single parents 8, 170–2
  for students 192
  see also Income Support; maternity payments
statutory maternity pay (SMP) 149–50, 151, 152–3
store cards, ease of obtaining 113–14
student grants 191
  information on 199
  Isobel's story 59–60
  Lisa's story 68, 69, 71
student loans 60, 189, 191, 192, 193, 199
students
  debt 59, 63, 66
  financial facts 191–2
  help and information for 199
  increasing numbers and financial hardship 189
  Isobel's story of financial hardship 59–67, 189–91
  Lisa's story of financial hardship 68–73
  see also graduates
suicide, Lisa's thoughts of 71, 72, 73
support
  Alice's lack of 57
  Emily's need for 49
  from Margaret's family 107, 108
  Lisa's lack of 70, 72
  Mary's need for 115, 117, 118
surviving debt
  addiction model 13
  experiences of 19–20
  Josephine's story 95–6, 98
  Margaret's story 109–11
  Mary's story 122–3
  PTSD model of 8–12
  Rebecca's attitude to business and 89
  role of control in 127

tax allowances 159, 170, 172–3
tax codes for graduates 193
telephone helplines 120–2, 128, 183
theft
  Mary's story 116, 117, 118
  to support Margaret's drug habit 11, 104, 107–8, 109, 110
Trading Standards Office 29, 30, 31
traditional role of women 38
  Alice's story 52–3, 58
  and divorce settlements 50–1, 58, 163–4
  Isobel's story 60–1
  Jennifer's story 22
  Josephine's story 91–2
  Margaret's story 100
training
  Josephine's homoeopathy training 91, 92, 93, 95
  Rebecca's business 79, 82

trauma *see* PTSD

unemployment 137–8
   dealing with mortgage payments 143
   Margaret's story 104
   see also dismissal; redundancy

validity of debts 130–3
violence within marriage
   Alice's story 52
   Emily's story 44–5
   Lisa's story 68
   Margaret's story 101

Wallet Watch 195
welfare benefits *see* state benefits

youth and community workers 75

Index by Judith Lavender